MEDITATIONS FOR EDUCATORS

MEDITATIONS
FOR EDUCATORS

by LOWRIE J. DALY, *S.J., Saint Louis University*
and Sister MARY VIRGENE DALY, *R.S.M.,*
College of Saint Mary

with an Introduction
by Very Reverend PAUL C. REINERT, *S.J.,*
President, Saint Louis University

SHEED AND WARD : NEW YORK

© *Sheed and Ward, Inc., 1965*

Library of Congress Catalog Card Number 65-20865

Imprimi Potest
    Linus J. Thro, S.J.
    Provincial
    Missouri Province

Nihil Obstat
    James T. Clarke, S.T.L.
    Censor Librorum
    April 20, 1965

Imprimatur
    ✠ *Jerome D. Hannan, D.D.*
    Bishop of Scranton
    April 27, 1965

The scriptural quotations in this book are from *The Holy Bible,* Confraternity Edition. Copyright 1962 by The Confraternity of Christian Doctrine.

Manufactured in the United States of America

To the Reader

These simple meditations are offered to those who like ourselves are administrators or teachers in modern religious congregations, in the hope that they be of some help in achieving the perfection for which we are all striving. We hasten to add that there is nothing very original in these thoughts. Yet, since they are based upon the everyday experience of modern religious, we hope that they may be of aid to all of us who combine the life of Martha and Mary and strive at least in some small degree to become "contemplatives in action."

LOWRIE J. DALY, S.J.

SISTER MARY VIRGENE DALY, R.S.M.

Contents

Contents   9

Introduction

A disturbing problem facing most religious men and women today is how to be very much 'in the world' but not 'of the world.' Faced with the ever more complicated apostolic tasks of teaching, caring for the sick and needy, and a myriad of other works, sisters, brothers and priests are increasingly concerned about the danger of losing that inner spirit which alone gives meaning to these external efforts. Of course, we all know the facile answer: cultivate a vigorous life of prayer. But most of us find this ability to speak to God *'ex abundantia cordis'* an accomplishment which requires a life-long struggle.

It is my impression that religious find relatively few meditation books that lend substantial help to their efforts to improve their life of prayer. Even today so many of these manuals are medieval in language and in their 'practical' applications. Rarely do their observations and exhortations ring true to the hard realities of modern, materialistic America. Our prayer life cannot flourish in a vacuum, far removed from the 'real' world in which we do our work for Christ, a world turned soft and satisfied by all the comforts and distractions that have pervaded even the cloister.

Never before was there greater need for all the aids we can make available to help religious achieve and maintain the peace and tranquillity which comes only from union with God.

Counteracting the materialistic attacks so violent and harmful to our prayer life today are, fortunately, the wonderful changes taking place in the liturgical life of the Church. In these fortunate modern times, religious and laity alike have an unprecedented opportunity to participate fully and personally in the mysteries of our redemption. If properly used, there can be no doubt about the salutary effects of our liturgical participation on our prayer life, since the very heart of the latter must be centered in the Divine Mystery of the Mass. Our own personal prayer life must be merged into the corporate worship of the people of God as they adore and serve their common Father. But these more active types of corporate participation, if they remain mere external acting, can harm rather than strengthen our prayer. They are futile unless they bring the individual soul into direct confrontation with his Lord and Redeemer. Corporate worship by the Church Militant is essential, but its essence consists in a union of the hearts and souls of many individuals, each of whom must bring his own spirit into the proper dispositions of praise, adoration, petition, and thanksgiving. Depending on the degree of divine charity in the participants, corporate worship is more or less perfect and acceptable in God's sight.

The materialism of our times, therefore, demands the availability of modern, effective aids to a vigorous prayer life.

Yet, the modern liturgical movement will not in itself
guarantee a sound, deepening union of the individual religious with our Blessed Lord. Hence, I am persuaded that
the book of meditations here presented will prove to be the
unique kind of modern aid that is so sorely needed. No
meditation book, of course, not even one as well written as
this by Father Daly and Sister Virgene, can guarantee to develop or strengthen the spirit of prayer in any soul. But such
meditations as herein suggested, combining the inspiring
thoughts of God in the Old and New Testaments with
practical considerations of the daily concerns of modern religious teachers and administrators, will surely be a welcome
addition to this undeveloped field in ascetical writing. *Meditations for Educators* is a new, effective means to the all-
important end—to prepare the way, as did John the Baptist,
for the entrance and acceptance of Christ.

God himself must always be the real agent in our prayer
life—not the writer of a book of meditations, not even the
words of the mystery which is being contemplated. God,
our Lord, must speak to the soul—and any ideas or helps
leading up to that experience fall short of being prayer in the
true sense. May this volume help us all to advance quickly
towards the day when Christ's desire for the fullness of prayer
in his apostles may be realized in us: ". . . . that they may
be one as we are one,—I in them and you in me" (John
17:22).

PAUL C. REINERT, S.J.
President
Saint Louis University

1

Seeking God in All Things

1st Prelude: Picture to yourself our Lord teaching and instructing his Apostles in preparation for their work of the ministry.

2nd Prelude: Ask for a deeper understanding of the relationship between your prayer and your apostolate.

St. Paul emphasized very clearly the importance of seeking God in all things.

> Therefore, whether you eat or drink, or do anything else, do all for the glory of God. (I Cor. 10:31)
> Whatever you do in word or in work, do all in the name of the Lord Jesus, giving thanks to God the Father through Him. (Col. 3:17)

For us who are combining the contemplative and active lives, striving to become "contemplatives in action," these words are very important indeed. To find God in all things is essential for us. Thus we sanctify the many actions of our busy lives; whether we teach or prepare for class, whether we counsel and advise, whether we work through the varied day of an administrator in educational or hospital work, in all our actions we must seek God. And if we seek him we shall find him. "Of you my heart speaks; you my glance seeks; your presence, O Lord, I seek." (Ps. 26:8) " 'Yes, when you seek me with all your heart, you will find me with you,' says the Lord." (Jer. 29:13)

St. Ignatius, writing for this type of contemplative-action, laid down the general ideal in his *Constitutions*.

> Let them seek God in all things, putting off as far as possible all love of creatures to place all their love in the Creator, loving Him in all His creatures, and all His creatures in Him, according to His most holy and divine will.[1]

And in reference to those who were in their studies, he gave the following advice.

> As our scholastics, considering their labors, cannot prolong their prayers, let them have recourse to the exercise of seeking God's presence in everything, in their conversations, their walks, in all that they see, taste, hear, and whatever else they do. For it is true that the Divine Majesty is in all things by His presence, His power, and His essence. Now this way of meditating,

[1] P. III, c. 1, n. 26. From A. Brou, S.J., *Ignatian Methods of Prayer,* published by the Bruce Publishing Company, 1949, p. 38.

of rising to God our Lord through all creatures is easier than that which raises us to the consideration of divine things that are more abstract and require a greater effort in making them present to us. It is an excellent exercise which disposes the soul for great visits from our Lord even in a short prayer. We can still endeavor to offer God, and that frequently, our studies and labors, considering that we accept them through love, without regard to our personal tastes, but merely to serve His Majesty to some extent, and to be of help to those for whom He died. . . .[2]

It is necessary for me to think over these words seriously. Have I been acting on such principles in my own religious life? Sometimes religious students set up a dichotomy in their spiritual lives and even allow their studies to become an obstacle to their increase in virtue when they are meant to be a help. The same may be said for the average round of our busy days after we have finished our novitiate and period of preparation for our work, and when we are engaged in the fullness of the apostolate to which God in his kindness has called us.

Let me examine my everyday actions carefully, let me review the daily routine of work and prayer and conversation to see whether or not I am seeking God in all my daily actions and duties. During my colloquies in this meditation let me make the sentiments of these verses my own.

[2] *Epistolae*, III, 507-510, June 1, 1551, translated in Brou, *op. cit.*, p. 39.

But may all who seek you (O Lord) exult and be glad in you, and may those who love your salvation say ever, "The Lord be glorified." Though I am afflicted and poor, yet the Lord thinks of me. You are my help and my deliverer, O my God, hold not back. (Ps. 39:17)

Those who love me I also love and those who seek me find me. . . . Happy the man watching daily at my gates, waiting at my doorposts; For he who finds me finds life. . . . (Prov. 8:17, 35)

2

Seeking God in My Work

1st Prelude: Listen to St. Paul saying, ". . . whether you eat or drink, or do anything else, do all for the glory of God" (I Cor. 10:31).

2nd Prelude: Ask for the grace to find God constantly in *your* apostolate.

We must apply the theory of finding God in all things to our own lives. This is not always easy to do. It requires practice, a lifetime of it! But it is essential for our vocation. It is the way in which God has called us to serve and to praise him. Any and every thing else must be secondary to that.

First of all let us consider *the things* we do each day. We might well begin with our prayer life since this is generally the first big section of our day after we get up. Did I ever total the amount of time that I put in at prayer each day? If I studied any branch of knowledge for as many hours each day, year in and year out, I would undoubtedly be an expert in it by now. Where do I stand in the efficiency of my prayer life? Am I seeking God there? Am I relating that prayer life to the other parts of my day in which all is to be done in the service of God? Do I usually find that after my prayer in the morning I am more ready and more willing to do the other work of the day? If not, then I had better examine the relationship between my prayer and my accomplishment of the will of God which is the be all and the end all of my whole religious life. "At dawn let me hear of your kindness, for in you I trust. Show me the way in which I should walk, for to you I lift up my soul." (Ps. 142:8)

Then let me carefully go through the various parts of my day. If it is devoted to teaching or study, administration or counselling, medical or nursing work, how am I seeking God in it? If I am happy in it, that is a very good sign; if I am not, I had better find out what the trouble is. Do I ever pause in the midst of a busy morning to rededicate my work? After all, the Morning Offering to the Sacred Heart *can* be said more than once a day! Do I habitually realize that the accomplishment today of God's will in my life is the greatest act that, as a rational being, I can perform? "Seek the Lord, while he may be found, call him while he is near." (Isa. 55:6) "Take delight in the Lord, and he will grant you your heart's requests." (Ps. 36:4)

There is another area of the day at which I might cast a glance of inspection—my recreation. Community recreation is not always pleasant, but when it isn't at least part of the trouble is due to me. For the smooth working of any cooperative project such as a school or hospital, the tone of a community's success can often be measured by its community recreation. And the reason is easy to learn. Generally speaking, the way we get to know and appreciate the members of the community with whom we live and work is by talking to them and by learning more about them—their ideals and their attitudes, their difficulties and their talents. "If thou wishest to be borne with, bear also with others." (Thomas à Kempis, *The Following of Christ,* Book II, Chapter III) Those who consistently absent themselves from normal community recreation only handicap themselves.

What is my attitude toward community recreation? Do I try to make it pleasant for others or simply go for my own enjoyment, seeking out only those whose attitudes and ideas are congenial to me? Do I ever consider that community recreation is a part of my apostolate; that "my neighbor" is a term that also includes the members of the community? "What ever you do, work at it from the heart as for the Lord and not for men, knowing that from the Lord you will receive the inheritance as your reward. Serve the Lord Christ." (Col. 3:23)

3

Conditions for Successful Prayer:
Generosity

1st Prelude: Picture to yourself our Lord at prayer.

2nd Prelude: Ask the grace to prepare well for prayer.

St. Margaret Mary gave this advice in regard to one's meditation:

> If you wish to make a good meditation, be faithful in mortifying yourselves, keep your minds in a state of deep recollection throughout the day. Commit no fault deliberately.

And in regard to the proper attitude for those making the *Exercises,* St. Ignatius says in his fifth annotation:

> It will much benefit him who is receiving the *Exercises* to enter upon them with a large heart and with liberality toward his Creator and Lord, offering all his desires and liberty to Him in order that His divine Majesty may make use of his person and of all he possesses according to His most holy will.

Although this direction is intended primarily for a retreatant, the advice in both quotations applies to our whole prayer life. We must be generous with God. And in return he will be most generous with us. It is a generosity which comes from deep love for the Master and for the fulfillment of his will. "If you love me, keep my commandments." (John 14:15)

A first test of our spirit of generosity might be to ask ourselves *why* we make our prayer. Do we go to prayer only to seek sensible consolations and enjoyment, or do we pray to fulfill the will of God? The spiritual writers tell us that we should expect dryness and desolation at times of prayer and on occasion even temptations; certainly we can expect wanderings of the mind. They need not have told us; we find it out quickly enough. It is precisely under such circumstances that we discover whether we are truly generous or not.

St. Ignatius has given us a bit of practical advice on the matter:

> . . . As in time of consolation it is easy and pleasant to remain the full hour in contemplation, so in time of desolation it is very difficult to complete it; wherefore, the exercitant, in order to go against the desolation and to overcome the temptation must always remain a short time beyond the full hour, so as to accustom himself not only to resist the enemy, but even to overthrow him.

There is a great deal of wisdom in this advice, but it is not always easy to follow. To fulfill the allotted time of prayer, whether it be an examination of conscience, meditation, or oral prayer, often calls for courage when things are not going easily, when our minds are distracted, when there is some duty which seems much more interesting waiting for us after the time of prayer. But it teaches us again that we go to prayer, as we go to all other things, to do God's will. If we accomplish that, we accomplish everything.

Let me examine my general attitude toward my prayer life. Do I habitually start my prayer with an offering of it to God to do his will? (The Morning Offering can easily be repeated and adapted to this purpose.) To praise, to reverence, to thank God, to beg forgiveness and help, these are the great motives of prayer. The more I can work them into the various parts of my daily prayer life, the more successful I shall be. And being generous with God is one way of making my prayer most effective. Then, too, the generosity with which I perform the various and at times difficult duties of my day carries over into my prayer life, just as a lack of generosity will have a weakening effect upon my general life of prayer.

Let me say slowly the following prayer, *Suscipe:*

Receive, O Lord, all my liberty. Take my memory, my understanding, and my entire will. Whatsoever I have or hold, Thou has given it; I give it all back to Thee and commit it wholly to be governed by Thy will. Thy love and Thy grace give unto me, and I am rich enough and ask for nothing more.

4

Conditions for Successful Prayer: Mortification

1st Prelude: Imagine our Lord making his prayer carefully, devoutly, attentively.

2nd Prelude: To beg earnestly for the grace to realize clearly the close connection between self-denial and successful prayer.

We note that St. Margaret Mary, in her advice on how to make a good meditation, stressed the need for being "faithful in mortifying" ourselves. St. Ignatius also strongly emphasized the need for mortification and self-denial for successful prayer. Whenever he spoke of prayer, he assumed that a person's passions were under control and "mortified." When a fellow religious once spoke of a person as "a man of great prayer," Ignatius immediately corrected him: "He is a very mortified man." And one of his most emphatic statements was, "A man who is truly mortified will find a quarter of an hour long enough to unite himself with God in prayer." It is not how long we pray, but what we do in that space of time.

Often enough the difficulty with this advice is not in the theory but in our practice of it. Due perhaps to the type of spiritual reading that many of us made in our novitiate days, the concepts of "penance" and "mortification" immediately conjure up the long fasts of the Fathers of the Desert and the "nightly vigils" of many of the early ascetics. Faced with the practical everyday life we lead and not having a desert nearby, we immediately lay aside the advice as something which is beyond our powers. Yet secretly we are often uneasy, because we fear that this means in effect that we are not really living up to the perfection demanded of us.

There is a twofold danger involved here. First of all, we may completely overlook the importance of *interior* mortification. After all, the purpose of mortification is to bring our passions and unruly emotions under control. We must ponder the meaning of mortification in its widest sense, taking into consideration that interior mortification which brings our passions under control, which detaches us more and more from all sin and disorder in our own lives; the mortification of immediate obedience, the denial of self-love in not always having the final word and the wittiest remark, in letting somebody else have the floor once in a while! These are very important in the conquest of self-love and pride, and we don't need a desert in which to practice them. The amount of self-denial involved in consistent community living is quite enough to bring us to very high perfection indeed. Thus we see that opportunities for self-denial are there already; we are the ones who fail to make use of them. "And he who does not take up his cross and follow me, is not worthy of me." (Matt. 10:38)

There is a great amount of self-denial in keeping silence "when it is to be kept," and when speaking, in talking as befits a person vowed to Christian perfection. For example, let me carefully go through my daily use of the senses God has given me and note the amount of mortification and self-denial which is connected with a right use of them. The tongue, the eyes, the ears—what tremendous opportunities are available each day in their correct use. Let me read carefully the following excerpt from the Constitutions of a modern religious order. It is an excerpt particularly fitted to the modern apostolic orders and it shows the amount of self-denial available in the proper use of the senses.

All must be exactly careful to guard the gates of their senses, especially their eyes, their ears, and their tongue, from all disorder, and to preserve themselves in true internal humility, showing it in silence when it is to be kept, and when they have to speak, in the circumspection and edification of their words, in the modesty of their countenance, gravity of their gait and whole carriage, without any sign of impatience or pride; procuring and wishing in all things to yield to others the better part, esteeming all in their hearts as their superiors, and giving them outwardly the honor and reverence which every one's state requires, with simplicity and religious moderation. And hence it will follow that considering one another they will increase in devotion and praise our Lord God, whom every one must strive to acknowledge in another as in His image.

Looking back over my daily actions do I find this to be a mirror of my conduct?

5

Conditions for Successful Prayer: Purity of Heart

1st Prelude: Hear our Lord saying to you, "Blessed are the pure of heart for they shall see God" (Matt. 5:8).

2nd Prelude: Beg insistently for a clear understanding of the many opportunities in your daily life which will aid purity of soul.

A fifteenth-century work on prayer, *De adhaerendo Deo,* tells us that "among all spiritual exercises, purity of heart in a certain manner claims the first place." And St. Thomas, in explaining what is meant by purity of heart, notes:

> There are two kinds of purity. One prepares us to see God; it cleans the heart of disordered affections and is developed in the soul by the virtues and the gifts (of the Holy Ghost) which pertain to the appetitive faculties. The other is a complement to this preparation for the vision of God: it detaches the mind from bodily phantasms and errors, and is the work of the gift of the understanding.[1]

[1] *Summa Theologica,* IIa IIae, q. 8, a. 7., as quoted in Brou, *op. cit.,* p. 71.

And we remember that St. Margaret Mary, in her advice on how to meditate well, warned us, "Commit no fault deliberately."

We remember, too, the frequent advice of Holy Scripture on the importance of purity of heart and soul, and the petitions of the Psalmist for this grace. "Who can ascend the mountain of the Lord, who may stand in his holy place? He whose hands are sinless, whose heart is clean, who desires not what is vain, nor swears deceitfully to his neighbor." (Ps. 23:3) "A clean heart create for me, O God, and a steadfast spirit renew within me." (Ps. 50:12)

The theory is clear enough; what may sometimes escape us is the practical aspect of this striving for purity of heart, particularly the fact that so much possibility lies within the framework of the prayer and activity that we do each day. How often does the subject of my meditation bring up the need for purity of heart, for singleness of affection. Every day I say various vocal prayers at different times, and how often do the subject of sorow of sin and the need for cleanness of heart come up by way of petition and request! Especially important in this matter is the opportunity I have when I make my examination of conscience. Then and there I beg God's forgiveness for my defects and resolve to achieve a greater freedom from sin and failures. How often do I attach this desire with my progress in prayer, with my success at my daily meditation? Yet they are closely related. "Happy is he whose fault is taken away, whose sin is cov-

ered. Happy the man to whom the Lord imputes not guilt, and in whose spirit there is no guile." (Ps. 31:1)

But purity of heart includes also a control of affections and desires, a detachment of heart which enables me to serve God alone! What a number of opportunities of achieving such detachment and control the daily round of duties affords us. There are so many things which demand our courage and our firm resolution to accomplish. Each of these can play its part in teaching us detachment and in securing for us the grace of a wholehearted service of God. Mortification and self-denial are closely related to purity of heart and control of desires. It brings us back once again to the *unity* that must permeate our whole religious life, to the realization that each part of it plays upon the other, and in each, and by each, we fulfill the will of God in our lives.

We must constantly remind ourselves that any departmentalization which sets up one part of our religious day as an autonomous and independent section having no relation to the rest is a real snare and a delusion. Perhaps in some ways it is *the* great snare that lies in wait for members of modern day religious orders. The modern apostolate is not a series of independent and unrelated desk drawers which one opens and shuts at different times. No, it is a continuous thing, the graces of prayer flowing into God's work which I am doing, and the work I am doing creating in me a deeper development of my prayer life.

Let us recall the important words of St. Paul:

And may the God of Peace himself sanctify you *completely,* and may your spirit and soul and body be preserved sound, blameless at the coming of our Lord Jesus Christ. He who called you is faithful and will do this. (I Thess. 5:23)

6

Helps to Meditation: Preparations

1st Prelude: Imagine to yourself our Lord making his prayer alone upon the mountain.

2nd Prelude: I want God's help to understand the importance of the acts preparatory to my meditation.

We generally select our meditation book or the material we wish for our prayer with some care, and we generally spend a certain amount of time the night before, preparing our meditation. If we don't, we usually find that things do not go so well with our prayer. But there are some additional helps to successful prayer which we may sometimes overlook. First of all, there is the control of our thoughts upon retiring. It's a good psychological trick to help us concentrate on our prayer the next morning. Although they did not have the benefits of modern psychological knowledge, the saints through the ages have given us good advice on such control. St. Ambrose, in the fourth century, thus directed the virgins at Milan:

I should wish that even when you have retired you frequently join the psalms to the Lord's Prayer, whether it be when you have just awakened, or before sleep has bound your limbs, so that, even at the beginning of your rest, sleep will find you free from care regarding worldly matters, and meditating on divine things.[1]

St. Bonaventure instructed his novices, before going to sleep, to "recite the psalms, meditate on some pious thought or picture Jesus crucified," and on awaking, to think again of the Crucified. St. Ignatius in the first Addition of the *Exercises* advised:

> ... After going to bed, when I want to go to sleep, to think for the space of a Hail Mary, of the hour when I have to rise, and for what purpose, summing up the Exercise which I have to make.

The monastic usage of the "Great Silence" after Compline is in line with this care for the morning prayer.

Having taken care of our last thoughts before sleeping, let us note the importance of control of thoughts and imagination upon arising. If we immediately begin to worry about the cares of the day and all its various problems or joys, we are apt to cause ourselves needless distractions. For this reason the saints have stressed the importance of turning our minds immediately to the prayer which we are shortly to make. Some people wake up quickly and others do not, but generally speaking most of us don't like to *get*

---

[1] *De Virginibus, Patrologia Latina,* 16, col. 225, as translated in Brou, *op. cit.,* p. 84.

up. Hence the need to encourage ourselves to begin that day's service of God. Here the Morning Offering can be a big help, and the use of short prayers, snippets from the psalms, or indulgenced aspirations don't weary us and yet they quite securely create an atmosphere of prayer conducive to a successful meditation.

On this point St. Ignatius, in line with the suggestions of St. Ambrose and St. Bonaventure, advises us to concentrate on what we are about to do.

> When I awake, not admitting other thoughts, immediately to turn my mind to that which I am going to contemplate in the first exercise . . . bringing myself to confusion for my many sins, proposing examples to myself, as if a knight were to stand before his King and all his court, covered with shame and confusion, because he had grievously offended him from whom he had received many gifts and favors.

The saint here applies the general rule to a specific meditation, and we can do the same to the subject of our meditation, varying the sentiments and thoughts with the liturgical season and with the subject of our meditation.

What care do I exercise to control my imagination and thoughts during this critical time before my meditation? "Hearken to my words, O Lord, attend to my sighing. Heed my call for help, my king and my God! To you I pray, O Lord: at dawn you hear my voice; at dawn I bring my plea expectantly before you." (Ps. 5:1 ff.)

7

Helps to Meditation: Preparations (II)

1st Prelude: Imagine yourself watching St. Paul as he writes these words to his Roman converts: "But in like manner the Spirit also helps our weakness. For we do not know what we should pray for as we ought, but the Spirit himself pleads for us with unutterable groanings" (Rom. 8:26).

2nd Prelude: Ask the grace to understand the importance of preparing yourself well for your prayer.

Do we ever stop to consider with what care we usually prepare ourselves for an important conference with this or that administrator or superior? When we have to make a proposal which means much to us, how carefully we work out the details and have our thoughts in good order so that our presentation will be as well done as possible. On the other hand, are we consistent and do we make a like and careful preparation when we have things to discuss with God?

When we go to pray, we go to place ourselves in contact with God and hence we should prepare ourselves for this. Thus it is natural that certain liturgical practices should have developed in connection with the recitation of the Office. Before beginning Matins, for instance, the *O God, come to my assistance,* the *O Lord, open my lips,* and the psalm *Come, let us praise the Lord with joy;* all these are aids to rouse the person to an appreciation of what he is about to do. The same is as true of mental prayer as of vocal. St. Theresa thus advises us:

> To pray properly one should begin by examining one's conscience, then recite the Confiteor and make the sign of the cross. Since you are alone, seek company. And what better company than that of the Master? Imagine you see our Lord close by.[1]

The general suggestions given us by spiritual writers and saints in regard to this immediate preparation for prayer come to three: to place ourselves in the presence of God; to humble ourselves before God; and to ask his help and grace.

With regard to the first, St. Ignatius thus summarizes the traditional advice in the Third Addition to his *Exercises.*

> I will stand for the space of a *Pater Noster* one or two paces from the place in which I am about to contemplate or meditate, and with my mind raised on high, consider how God our Lord sees me, and I will make an act of reverence and humiliation.

[1] *Way of Perfection,* Chapter 26, as quoted in Brou, *op. cit.,* p. 87.

Once we realize to whom we are about to speak, it is quite natural that we, poor little creatures, should adore our God. "And entering into the house they found the child with Mary his mother, and falling down they worshipped him." (Matt. 2:11) And it is just as natural that we confess ourselves for what we are—sinners, people on whom God has lavished his gifts and who have often made a poor return on the investment.

We are naturally then led to ask God's help and grace, "Lord, teach us to pray." We can choose our own prayer for this or make one up. St. Francis de Sales encourages us to select "short and burning phrases from the psalms," and we note the development of the prayer *Aperi* before the recitation of the Office. St. Ignatius again summarizes the advice for us.

> The preparatory prayer is to ask our Lord for grace that all my intentions, actions, and operations may be ordained purely to the service and praise of His divine majesty.[2]

This is not only a plea for help but a direction of our prayer. Here as in our whole lives we are working for the glory of God, not for our own comfort or enjoyment. "Our Father Who art in Heaven, hallowed be thy name, thy kingdom come, thy will be done . . ." A prayer we could sometimes use at the beginning of our meditation is the Morning Offering.

[2] Third Addition to the *Exercises,* First Week, First Exercise.

In a letter written to the Bishop of Osma, St. Theresa also gives us some advice that we can think over and see how close it comes to what we have been doing as immediate preparation for our meditation.

After having made the sign of the cross, accuse yourself before God of the least sins committed since your last confession. Conceive a detachment from all things as though you were going to die that day, that very hour. Repent sincerely of these faults, and, as a penance, recite the psalm *Miserere*. Then say: "I come to Your school, O Lord, to learn and not to teach. I wish to speak with Your Majesty, although I am but dust and ashes and a miserable worm of the earth." Then say again: "Deign, O Lord, to manifest Your power in me even though I am but a poor insect." Offer yourself as a perpetual holocaust. Imagine Jesus Christ crucified before the eyes of your soul and those of your body. Contemplate Him, and study Him in detail in the calm and love of your soul.[3]

[3] Quoted from Brou, *op. cit.*, p. 87.

8

Imagination in Meditation

1st Prelude: Hear our Lord speaking to the people and note his use of stories and parables.

2nd Prelude: Ask for the grace which you wish and hope for: to make good use of the talents God has given *you*.

Most of us have read the warnings of certain spiritual writers against the overuse of the imagination in our prayer life, of the dangers and illusions which an over-wrought imagination can conjure up for the imprudent religious. These warnings are to be heeded. On the other hand, it sometimes seems that we tend to condemn any use of our imaginative faculties in our prayer life. This is to go to the other extreme.

All we have to do is glance at the TV set or pick up any newspaper or magazine to see the tremendous emphasis which is given today to an appeal to our imaginations. Anybody who doubts the helpfulness of a first prelude to our meditations has only to watch one or two commercials on TV to see and understand what an aid the imagination can be to effective resolution. The commercial has a single purpose: to make the observer resolve to buy that product! It does not take much observation, either, to convince ourselves that human imagination is used with great effect in many things around us, and we immediately wonder if it can be helpful in our prayer life.

It can. The prayer life of Christendom from the thirteenth century (or even from the twelfth) to the sixteenth is proof of this. For example, consider the commentary of St. Aelred of Rievaux, in the twelfth century, on the words of the Canticle of Canticles.

> ... I have found him who my soul loveth. I will hold him and I will not let him go. Hold him, O Gentle Lady, hold him whom you love, cast yourself upon his neck, embrace him, kiss him, and by your multiplied caresses make up for the three days' absence. "My Son, why have you done so to us? Behold your father and I have sought you sorrowing." Once again I ask you, O Gentle Lady, why were you sorrowful? Not because of hunger or thirst, or the privations that you feared for the Child. You knew that he was God. You lamented only because he had taken away from you, even for a moment, the unspeakable delights of his presence. He is so sweet, the Lord Jesus, to those who relish him, so beautiful to those who see him, so gentle to those who embrace him, that a very brief absence causes a great pain.[1]

[1] *De Jesu doudenni*, n. 8, *Patrologia Latina*, 184, col. 854, as translated in Brou, *op. cit.*, p. 133.

Here is another example, this one from the *Vita Christi* of Ludolph the Carthusian, a book which had a great effect upon St. Ignatius of Loyola.

... For the life of Christ has all that a sinner needs as long as he lives on this earth of darkness and misery. Come to Jesus, my brethren, with a recollected heart, and following him through all the days of his life, taste the abundant fruits of consolation and of doctrine which each one of his words and actions offers you. ...

And in order that this meditation be profitable to you, make the words and actions of Jesus present to your mind. Let what happened centuries ago renew itself before you. Listen to Jesus, see him as he walks, as he sits; let his voice sound in your ears. Cultivate familiarity with the dear Master, look upon his venerable countenance which inspires respect and love, those eyes bright with divinity and mercy, that aspect, that bearing, full of sweetness and gravity.

Then let your imagination represent that blessed land made glorious by so many prodigies. ... See the cave at Bethlehem ... the poor house at Nazareth. ...[2]

St. Ignatius lived at a time when this type of imaginative meditation had reached full development, and he synthesized it in simple lines and used it as one of the forms of meditation in his *Exercises*. So that our memory, under-

[2] Brou, *op. cit.,* p. 134.

standing and will can get to work upon a particular event in the gospel, he advises that we pay heed to the persons, the words and the actions.

We use our imagination to help us. St. Francis de Sales notes that the imagination can be of little help to those who are far advanced in perfection, but for "us others who are still in the valley, I think it would be best to use all our tricks." And he explains his ideas more fully in his letter to the Baroness de Chantal (*Oeuvres*, xiii, 162).

I can well ask myself if I make a proper use of my imagination, especially if I am gifted with an active one. Do I try to aid myself by carefully imagining the historical scene; and when my imagination and thoughts wander off, bring them back by recalling the scene? This is what the "first prelude" is intended to do. If we find it useful, fine. If not, we can simply pass it by. True, the imagination is after all but a poor tool, and St. Francis warns the Baroness not to spend considerable time at it. But if recalling the "first prelude" keeps me from going to sleep during prayer time, I can well use it!

9

The Colloquy in Our Meditation

1st Prelude: Picture to yourself the Apostles engaged in earnest conversation with our Lord.

2nd Prelude: To clearly understand the importance of frequent colloquies in your morning prayer.

We are all familiar with the word "colloquy" which we have often noted in our meditation books and in our spiritual reading, but have we ever sat down seriously to consider the importance of the colloquy in our own prayer? Spiritual writers constantly tell us that "prayer is a conversation with God." The other parts of meditation, such items as preparation, topics or points, preludes, our use of our understanding and will, are all to bring us to a "conversation with God." And this should be our normal prayer. All of these aspects of meditation help us to concentrate on the matter before us and motivate us to the love of God.

At some time or other each of us has had to console someone who has lost mother or father, wife or husband, and we must have noted how every thought of their loved one's kindness to them, the memory of past companionship

44

brought a new onrush of sorrow and grief. When we con-sider the great and constant goodness of God towards us in so many ways each day, this too should bring, almost in-stantaneously, affections of sorrow for our past sins, grati-tude and thanks for the goodness of God, and so on. Why is it that these affective prayers come so slowly to us? Perhaps because we think about God's goodness to us so little.

Our affectionate outcries to God can be put in our own words or in the words of prayers long familiar to us. We can find sentiments which exactly fit our desires and our feelings in the simple words of the psalms. That is probably the reason why the psalms have always been a main source of the Church's prayer—they are the sincere, simple and ordi-nary affections of a devout soul. They put in simple fashion the usual but deep emotions and affections of every human being toward God—thanks, sorrow, love, adoration, and petition.

That is what the colloquy does for our prayer. It is the climax, the culmination of the various preparations which we make, starting with the control of the imagination and including the exercise of the intellect. And when anybody achieves this conversation with Christ, that person should continue in it according to the measure of God's grace given him or her. Without such colloquies our prayer be-comes more or less of a type of spiritual reading or an intellectual exercise, but it ceases to be real prayer in the sense of a conversation with God. Do I really believe this?

Let me just for the moment examine the last five meditations I made during the past week. What part did colloquies play in them? How often in meditation did I find myself speaking freely and intimately with our Lord, praising him, thanking him, asking him for a special favor? (People don't generally go to sleep while engaged in conversation!) Discussing this or that weakness or failure, perhaps some person whom it is my duty and privilege to teach or to guide, can well form a part of my conversation with God. Let me converse now with our Lord about my present and past use of the colloquy in my meditation. Above all let me promise him to do better in the future.

The various acts of confidence of Psalm 30 should be mine.

> In you, O Lord, I take refuge; let me never be put to shame. In your justice rescue me, incline your ear to me, make haste to deliver me! . . . I will rejoice and be glad of your kindness, when you have seen my affliction and watched over me in my distress . . . How great is the goodness, O Lord, which you have in store for those who fear you . . . Blessed be the Lord whose wondrous kindness he has shown me . . .

10

Colloquies Should be Frequent

1st Prelude: Listen to the Apostles engaged in earnest conversation with our Lord: "Lord, teach us to pray" (Luke 11:1).

2nd Prelude: To clearly understand the importance of frequent colloquies during your morning prayer.

Spiritual writers tell us that the colloquies in our meditations should be made to our Lord or to the saints *as vividly present to us*. They are to be like conversations, not as if we were shouting to some far off person beyond the clouds who does not really know us and is not really interested in us. For this purpose I must make my acts of faith, realizing how God sees me present before him; picturing myself standing before our Lord or his Blessed Mother, earnestly telling them of my hopes and ambitions, my problems and my desires, begging them to help me with the supernatural helps without which I can do nothing.

Beyond these general directions it is difficult to see what one may add. Conversation is a two-way street. One must be able to listen as well as to speak. Our Lord has things to

47

make clear to us, things to inspire us to do so that our
service of him will be better that day. We have all made
meditations on certain important subjects many times in
our religious life, and so very often the matter of the day's
meditation is not at all new to us. Still, as these subjects
become a part of our thinking, as they become firm principles imbedded in our way of acting and judging, so it
should be easier for us to rise from them to the various
colloquies with our Lord.

For instance, how often we have made a meditation
about our Lord born for us in a stable! It should be easier
each time for us to enter into a conversation with him,
asking him how it is that he who is the Creator has come to
make himself man. Why it is that he should come thus into
his creation without comforts, while I have so many? Why
he has so few friends, and I so many? Why I am surrounded
by modern conveniences, while he hasn't even a cradle?
And so I pass on then to consider what I have done for him
in the past . . . what I am doing for him at the present . . .
what I hope to accomplish for him today. I can scarcely
think on such things without some acts of faith or hope or
love, without sorrow and gratitude, without in a word making a colloquy.

Spiritual writers also tell us of the importance of *ending
our meditation with a colloquy*. It is an important point,
they tell us, to conclude with this colloquy, even though
the meditation has not gone well, even though our mind has
been distracted with a thousand things, even when we have

awakened almost at the end of the meditation time to find ourselves slumbering instead of praying. As we come to the end of our conversation with God we once more sum up the thoughts and desires of our meditation, much as we do when we come to the end of an important conversation with someone. We renew our resolutions to mend this or that matter, to make this day a better day in God's service than yesterday. We once more renew our various acts of faith and hope and charity, we once more beg earnestly for the grace which we desire from this meditation.

The psalms very often afford us a way of expressing our thoughts and desires, but it is well to end the colloquy with a formal prayer like the Our Father. This is the perfect prayer, taught us by our Lord himself and it contains the chief petitions which a creature should ask of his Creator, an adopted son of his Heavenly Father. These are the petitions which should be the driving ambitions of our lives and which we should try to achieve in our work and prayer and suffering *this* very day.

11

Our Colloquies—About What?

1st Prelude: Imagine to yourself your patron saint engaged in earnest conversation with our Lord.

2nd Prelude: That colloquies with our Lord and his saints may become more and more a part of your normal prayer life.

When one asks what should be the matter or content of the colloquies during meditation, one is really asking what one should talk about with our Lord. Obviously this is a personal matter and everyone has to answer that for himself or herself. Still, some things can be suggested.

First of all, there is the second prelude of the meditation, or whatever it is that I wish to gain from my prayer with God *this* morning. Certainly that should be one of the things about which I shall speak, asking our Lord how a certain virtue can be made a part of my life, how I can secure that patience which I see to be so necessary for my own apostolate. Then I can naturally pass on to the various affections which such a petition will call forth—sorrow that I have made such a botch of this in the past, gratitude for the many virtuous acts which God has enabled me to perform despite my weakness, laziness, and lack of real interest in the spiritual life. The standard petition of so many of our meditations—that "we may know our Lord more clearly, love him more dearly and imitate him more nearly"—is in effect a summary of our whole spiritual life. "Now this is everlasting life, that they may know thee, the only true God and him who thou hast sent, Jesus Christ." (John 17:3)

We have our dull days. We also have our dull meditations. In order to avoid these it is well to have some standard colloquies to which we can turn when things are not going well with the meditation, when our mind seems a race track of distractions. The colloquy may take the form of a definite formula of devotion, some prayer to the Sacred Heart for example, which sums up in itself our aspirations and deepest affections. To express our aspirations and desires we may turn to that sentence from the psalms which has become a frequent refuge of ours or to some prayer from the liturgy of the Mass or the Divine Office in which we have often found strength and help.

But above all the matter of our colloquy should be our own. We should feel free to choose according to the meditation at hand, according to our own problems and joys of the day. We should take into account the particular state of our own soul and pray to God in one way when things are "going well," and in another way when we are given the privilege of sharing the suffering of our Master. We must always remind ourselves (because very often we really

don't believe it) that consolation is no measure of the
efficacy or real value of our prayer and that a few minutes
of aridity courageously accepted is very likely worth an
hour of consoling prayer.

We all have read of the great trials of God's chosen ones,
some of whom passed long years in dry and arid prayer,
giving all the while great glory to God. Yet on the other
hand, before we judge that dryness in prayer is such a trial,
let us diligently consider whether we have made our preparation for meditation well and whether we have really tried
hard to pray. The sources of dryness in our prayer may lie
as close as the unopened meditation book or the carelessly
omitted preparations for successful prayer.

Let me examine my use of the colloquy in prayer and see
whether or not I give thought to this part of my meditation.
Do I consistently strive to turn my prayer into conversation
with God? "Only in God is my soul at rest; from him comes
my salvation. He only is my rock and my salvation, my
stronghold; I shall not be disturbed at all . . . Only in God
be at rest, my soul, for from him comes my hope." (Ps.
61:1)

12

*The Importance of
the Examination of Conscience*

1st Prelude: Listen carefully to the words of our Lord: "Blessed are the pure of heart for they shall see God."

2nd Prelude: Ask for the grace to clearly understand the need for great purity of conscience and the further grace to do something about obtaining it, by a right use of the Examination of Conscience.

Sometimes we forget how old in monastic tradition is the practice of the examination of conscience. In the fourth century, St. Anthony, rightly considered the "Father of monasticism," stressed this point to those hermits who came to him seeking perfection. Cassian, whose works are so important in the history of Christian monasticism, also emphasized its importance. St. Bernard and St. Bonaventure did the same in the medieval period. St. Ignatius at the beginning of modern history so warmly advocated it that largely through his influence it has entered into the rules of most modern congregations. Indeed the modern Code of Canon Law now legislates for all clerics: "Ordinaries of places shall see to it that all clerics daily examine their conscience" (Can. 125).

What have I done in my life about a point so consistently stressed by the spiritual experts? Do I consider it of importance or is it the first thing that is put off if the schedule is tight? What am I doing about it today? "Be watchful and diligent in the service of God, and often think this over: What have you come hither for, and why have you left the world? Was it not to live for God?" Continue prayerfully this 25th Chapter of Book I of the *Imitation of Christ*.

St. John Chrysostom pointed out two good reasons for the use of the practice of examination of conscience. It prepares us for the next day because we note the mistakes we made today and resolve not to make the same ones tomorrow. This will be a check upon our conduct. And during the day itself, the fact that we are going to audit our conduct will help us to overcome temptation, for we know that we will have to render an account to ourselves that very day. Even the pagan philosopher Pythagoras taught his followers to have two times set aside during the day, one in the morning and the other in the evening, to check up on their conduct and progress. He suggested three good questions: What have I done? How have I done it? What have I left undone that I ought to have done?

And I, with all the help of faith, with the aid of the rules and regulations of my own order, the example of those around me—how have I used this key to spiritual perfection? Do I have to say of my soul what Proverbs says of the vineyard of the lazy man? "I passed by the field of the sluggard, by the vineyard of the man without sense; and behold! it was all overgrown with thistles; its surface was covered with nettles, and its stone wall broken down." (Prov. 24:30) Does this comparison fit me? What have I done about this practice in the past? What am I doing about it now? Maybe I have to say truthfully:

> Have mercy on me. O God, in your goodness; in the greatness of your compassion wipe out my offense. Thoroughly wash me from my guilt and of my sin cleanse me. For I acknowledge my offense, and my sin is before me always. Against you only have I sinned, and done what is evil in your sight—that you may be justified in your sentence. . . .

Let me continue to recite slowly and prayerfully this great act of contrition, Psalm 50.

13

The Value of the Particular Examination of Conscience

1st Prelude: Picture to yourself our Lord saying to you: "Blessed are the clean of heart for they shall see God."

2nd Prelude: The grace to clearly understand the importance of the particular examination of conscience in your own life.

The importance of the particular examination in a program for constant spiritual progress can hardly be exaggerated. St. Ignatius of Loyola, one of the greatest advocates of this practice, was satisfied if all that could be taught some persons who made the Spiritual Exercises was the practice of the particular and general examinations of conscience and a frequent use of the Sacraments. Today we are very conscious of budgets and bookkeeping. The necessity of balancing our accounts is always before us. The good businessman keeps a strict account of every transaction; otherwise he can scarcely hope to succeed in the highly competitive world in which he works. We who seek spiritual perfection can never forget that we too are in a very competitive market. The World, the Flesh, and the Devil are excellent salesmen; they are always on the job—selling sin. And often to us.

Do I really understand the need for purity of conscience in my own life? Yet how often do I preach it to others! Sin in my life is the negation of everything I stand for—and yet how often does it occur! The particular examination of conscience has the great merit of pinning me down to a specific problem or the practice of a certain virtue. It makes me do something about it *this* morning, *this* afternoon. If I do not review my day, I do not really know whether the day has been a spiritually successful one for me. If I do not check upon my success or failure in avoiding sin, I do not have an adequate knowledge of my real love and service of God—which is the reason why I exist, the reason why I am in the business of being a religious. A stuttering salesman needs to cure himself if he desires success; a bad-tempered religious had better check on the time, persons, and occasions when his or her temper got out of control.

In thinking of these matters let me make my own the prayer of Psalm 37, reading it slowly and prayerfully: "O Lord, in your anger punish me not, in your wrath chastise me not . . ." And let me ask earnestly for the grace of this meditation.

The particular examination of conscience is a great help to self-knowledge. An American literary figure once said that there were six people really engaged in a conversation between any two people. There is the person I think I am, the person my conversant thinks I am, and the person I really am; and three more on his side!

People who know themselves well are humble people; in fact, they can scarcely be any other kind! To take on one of our weaknesses of character and attempt to remedy it soon teaches us that the supernatural life really is above nature; that one cannot do anything without God's help; that our Lord's remark to the Apostles at the Last Supper, "without me you can do nothing" (John 15:6), does apply to each one of us. As we struggle to implant some virtue more firmly into our everyday life, as we strive to get along better with a certain person or job or assignment, as we chalk up our successes and failures each day for some weeks, we quickly become aware that we are really and truly in need of God's grace to make the slightest progress in our Spiritual Life.

Read prayerfully Chapter 7 of Book I of the *Imitation of Christ*, and ask for the grace of this meditation.

But the practice of the particular examination should not become a worry. One should practice it courageously and serenely, not fretting oneself or torturing the conscience. Indeed, a serious error that many make in the practice of the Particular Examen is to spend all the time in counting up the mistakes and relatively little time in asking God for forgiveness and help. Thus it is true that some may misunderstand this splendid means to self-knowledge and misuse this aid to spiritual progress by making it merely an adding machine of their faults. Nevertheless, it seems that many more religious fail in the other direction—by not using it seriously or not using it at all. It has been well said that the last place where the devil of tepidity rests is upon the Particular Examen booklet.

Let me prayerfully repeat Psalm 37 again and ask our Lord for the grace of this meditation: "O Lord, all my desire is before you; from you my groaning is not hid . . . Because for you, O Lord, I wait; you, O Lord, my God, will answer . . ."

14

Making the Particular Examen

1st Prelude: Imagine to yourself our Lord patiently instructing the people.

2nd Prelude: Ask for the grace to use the Particular Examen in your life.

The characteristics of the particular examination of conscience in themselves teach us much about its successful practice. First of all it must be *particular*. A resolution for making one's examination on "just being perfect" won't get anyone very far. It must be particular, it has to be about something definite. If we have (and who doesn't!) obvious faults or weaknesses which continually cause ourselves and others difficulty, the materials are already at hand for us. For example, if from our confessions and the attitude of members of our community we know that our temper is constantly getting in the way of our spiritual progress, then we should begin immediately with that. It's true that sins of temper may often be "only venial sins," but they can also often make life a Hell for those with whom we work.

The particular examination covers a part of a day or at most the whole day. If possible, it is better to limit it to this

morning or this afternoon. Such a short time encourages us
to watch over ourselves carefully at least for that long!
When we notice that we have fallen into the very temptation which we were working against, then is the time to
make a quick act of contrition and renew our resolution.
This can be done quietly and without anyone even noticing
it. The renewal once again brings into the focus of our
attention the purpose we have in mind.

In addition the successful practice of the examination
requires that we mark down our progress or lack of it during that morning or that afternoon and then compare it
with what happened the previous day, and after a week, to
check and see whether or not this week has been more
succcessful than last week. Thus the examination requires a
strong determination of the will and a constant vigilance.
We have to be on the alert always. As St. Peter warns us in
words which the Church has inserted into Compline: "Be
sober, be watchful! For your adversary the devil, as a roar-
ing lion, goes about seeking someone to devour" (I Peter
5:8).

It is true then that the whole of the particular examination always hinges upon our resolving, our praying, our
watching, our examining, and our comparing. But if we
want success in any field of endeavor, we have to go about
it in such ways. The business of the spiritual life requires the
same care that any other business does. And we must always remember that *we have made perfection the business
of our life.*

Still, the examination of conscience does not necessarily

have to fight directly against a defect. One may get rid of a defect or fault of character by implanting the opposite virtue. For instance, a person given to criticism (which seems to be the common recreation of some religious) may fight such a fault directly by concentrating upon the persons, places or events which he or she knows to be occasions of this weakness. Or such a one might determine to cultivate the habit of speaking kindly about everyone, of praising them instead of blaming them. This would be accomplished by noting the number of acts of such virtue that one had practiced during a morning or afternoon. Much depends upon the individual, and the freedom to choose this or that approach in the use of the particular examination should always be preserved. Sometimes a negative, sometimes a positive approach might work better; sometimes a varied one aids constant vigilance.

The use of brief indulgenced prayers in connection with the particular examination is of great help. A prayer which has some connection with the fault to be removed or the virtue to be stressed might be used, such as, "Jesus, meek and humble of heart, make my heart like unto thine." This not only recalls to mind the fact that one is striving to overcome pride in a special area, but it emphasizes the need for supernatural grace to achieve any spiritual progress at all. And it will bring us this grace if we use it.

Recall the words of Psalm 70, a prayer for perseverance: "In you, O Lord, I take refuge; let me never be put to shame . . ."

15

The General Examination of Conscience

1st Prelude: Hear our Lord as he emphasizes the words, "Blessed are the clean of heart, for they shall see God" (Matt. 5:8).

2nd Prelude: What I want from this meditation—the grace to understand and use the general examination of conscience.

It is sometimes forgotten that the general examination of conscience, as usually made, is really a prayer. First of all there is the act of *thanksgiving* with which it opens. We are all aware of the evil of ingratitude, but we become much more aware of it when someone does not thank *us* for a favor we have done. Sometimes it upsets our whole day! Yet how often do we thank God for the great favors he has bestowed upon us throughout our lives?

If we practice the general examination faithfully (once, or better, twice a day), we shall be sure of thanking God for his goodness to us. And we shall be wise to single out some special favors of that day or week for which we are particularly grateful. Let me make my own the words and sentiments of Psalm 64: "To you we owe our hymn of praise, O God, in Sion; To you must vows be fulfilled, you who hear prayers . . ."

The second point of the exercise is a prayer for light and help. Once more we make clear to ourselves that the business of our life is a supernatural one. We need God's help to make the slightest progress in the real business of our life. The third part consists of the examination of our thoughts, words, and actions of the day thus far.

A general examination can be made upon an hour by hour basis, or upon the various actions of our day, such as our prayer, our recreation, our study, our administrative duties, our classes, etc. If there is any outstanding defect that we have fallen into that morning or afternoon, we may be sure that we shall remember it. Not too much time should be spent upon this part of the exercise, rather we should concentrate on the portions which follow.

Our contrition for our defects and sins and our resolution to change ourselves for the better are most important. A comparison of the favors which God continually bestows upon us with the record of our own failings and ingratitude aids us in making a sincere act of contrition. The act of contrition should include not only the sins and defects of that day but those of our whole life as well. "Happy is he whose fault is taken away, whose sin is covered." (Ps. 31:1)

The resolution of amending our lives should be specific

and tied in with the particular examination of conscience, and should be made for *this* morning or *this* afternoon. We are warned not to base judgment of the sincerity of our sorrow upon a feeling or sensible emotion; but we should also warn ourselves that if our resolutions of amendment are watery and never have any effect on our conduct we can well wonder about the sincerity of our sorrow.

Sometimes religious fail to get much out of the practice of the examination of conscience because they spend most of the time allotted to the exercise in counting up their faults, and then pass over the acts of contrition and amendment quickly. The time is over before they can really be sorry for their sins! We must be sincerely sorry for our faults, and must take time out to be sure that we are. If we complain that we seldom make real progress in overcoming our defects, we should examine our use of the exercise to see if we really take time to make sincere acts of contrition and whether we are truly sorry for our sins. If we are sincerely sorry, our purpose of amendment will surely be effective. We do not easily do that which we really abhor! Grief for the past and purpose of amendment for the future go hand in hand. What is true of the general examination of conscience is true also of our use of the particular examen: sorrow and purpose of amendment are the two chief things; if we do these well, we shall unquestionably make spiritual progress and bring our faults under control. It will help me to reread sometimes the seventh treatise, "On the Examen of Conscience," in A. Rodriquez, *Practice of Perfection and Christian Virtues,* Vol. I.

Let me repeat slowly the great psalm of contrition, Psalm 50. "Have mercy on me, O God, in your goodness; in the greatness of your compassion wipe out my offense . . ."

16

*Examination of Conscience
for Educators: Administrators*

1st Prelude: Imagine that you are present as our Lord instructs the Apostles and disciples about their future work.

2nd Prelude: Beg of our Lord the grace to become more like him *by means* of your administrative work.

Whether my work is both administrative and instructive or entirely administrative, it might pay me to consider briefly some of the characteristics I should cultivate as an administrator. First let me ask myself how strongly the virtue of charity is evidenced in my administrative work; the kind of charity St. Paul described. "Charity is patient, is kind; charity does not envy, is not pretentious, is not puffed up . . . bears with all things . . . endures all things." (I Cor. 13:8) Do I strive to achieve this kind of charity in my work? Does it become practical in my attitude toward those who are my subordinates? Am I available and easy to consult or do I set up a series of secretarial blocks that make it almost impossible for others to consult me? Do I have office hours for the faculty as well as for chance callers?

Charity is *patient*. Is this characteristic of my attitude toward those whom I direct? Do I encourage them or discourage them? Sometimes administrators are accused of having one set of rules of politeness, interest, and affability for outsiders, and quite another for their own faculty and school personnel. Am I entirely free of such a fault? Do my teachers really like to consult me? If not, perhaps I had better investigate this matter thoroughly. In my administrative work, whether with students, faculty, or personnel, do I give evidence of Christ-like conduct? Am I as prompt in keeping my appointments and engagements as I demand others to be? Do I consistently strive to treat and deal with others as Christ dealt with those who came to consult him?

All administrators experience a certain amount of criticism. Most of them get to know that this is more or less inevitable. In any case there is generally a considerable amount of this unasked-for penance involved in administration, and perhaps I have found this to be quite true in my own work. What have I done about gaining the most from such difficulties? The daily acceptance of such trials—which I can make when I say my Morning Offering—will help me greatly in achieving perfection. For I must continually tell myself that it is precisely in the difficult duties of *today* that my perfection is gained, that *there* are my real opportunities to praise and reverence and serve God. Let me think back over the events of the past few days and see if any opportunities have slipped by without my realizing their value.

During my colloquies let me say the prayer *Suscipe*.

Take, O Lord, and receive all my liberty, my memory, my understanding, and my entire will. Whatever I have or hold, Thou hast given me; I restore it all to Thee and surrender it wholly to be governed by Thy will. Give me only Thy love and Thy grace, and I am rich enough and ask for nothing more.

17

Examination of Conscience for Educators: Teachers

1st Prelude: Observe our Lord teaching in the temple, surrounded by people—some interested, some listless, some antagonistic.

2nd Prelude: To beg earnestly for the grace to imitate Christ in your work for him.

It might pay to give myself a brief examination of conscience regarding my own teaching. Such little, seemingly little, items as punctuality, the beginning and ending of my classes on time, are worth considering! What is my usual attitude toward my students, whether they are in first grade or graduate school—is it one of patience and kindness? Can I say that I am always just toward all those in my classes, that I play no favorites, that I never allow my dislikes to become known and evident? A good teacher never becomes sarcastic or bullying—if he or she does, far more is lost than gained.

What of my class preparation? Are my classes as well prepared as I can make them? What kind of reading do I do to keep up on the material which I profess to teach? Do I ever pray about my teaching duties? Do I pray often for my students? Do I ever think about the great privilege of teaching, about the possibilities offered me to form the character of men and women whose influence may be extremely important in the next generation? Or has the whole business become merely a rat race in which I find little real interest?

Maybe I should think over some of the things a good teacher should *not* do! A good teacher should never ridicule a pupil's attempts at achievement; nor make sarcastic remarks about any particular nationality or color or creed; nor reprimand a student or blame one hastily; nor refuse to listen to a student's explanation; nor find fault or nag continually at students; nor refer to personal eccentricities of pupils. A good teacher will bestow praise where it is due and will not fail to bring out the good points in a pupil's work. We must always remember that the golden rule applies here as well: don't do to your pupils what you would not wish done to yourself.

At times all teachers feel discouraged. But even Socrates was not always successful! Sometimes the dull routine of semester after semester wears down the most optimistic, and a day with forty or fifty bright young things can leave one with only a few remnants of vim, vigor and vitality. Teaching the same things and correcting the same mistakes day after day can take the inspiration out of the tasks we are assigned. At this juncture let me think of our Lord's patient work with the difficult people with whom he had to deal day after day. Some of them were hostile, most of them were indifferent, and all of them were difficult to teach.

In my colloquies let me affirm once more my intention to the Lord: "I will teach transgressors your ways and sinners shall return to you" (Ps. 50:15). And let me remember that "those who lead the many to justice shall be like the stars forever" (Dan. 12:3).

18

Prayer and the Apostolate

1st Prelude: Imagine that you are accompanying our Lord as he goes about the countryside preaching and teaching the people.

2nd Prelude: I want the grace to understand clearly the relationship between my prayer and my apostolate.

We are all familiar with the usual question asked about the relative values of the active and the contemplative life. A customary answer has been that the first place is to be awarded to the contemplative life, the second to the active. The conversation of our Lord and Martha (Luke 11:41) has been interpreted in this way and the "contemplative" Mary is said to have chosen the better part.

It is interesting to note that St. Thomas Aquinas (d. 1274), more than seven centuries ago, did *not* follow precisely that generalization. He added that higher than either the simple active or the simple contemplative life was a life which combined the values of both. He explained that there is an interior activity which tends to purify the soul and develop the virtues in the purgative and illuminative ways

73

and then in the unitive way to lead to contemplation, and an exterior activity which is apostolic and includes preaching, the administration of the sacraments, and teaching. As he wrote: "For of itself charity appears stronger in the person who, not seeking consolation in divine contemplation, is intent on God's glory through the conversion of sinners. Even in human friendship, a true friend seeks more the good of his friend than the pleasure of his presence . . ." (*Commentary on the Sentences,* III, Dict. 35, q. 1 a. r, solut. 3).

Later on in his *Summa* St. Thomas noted that there is an active life which proceeds from the fullness of contemplation, such as that engaged in teaching and preaching, and that such a life is more excellent than simple contemplation, for it is better to give to others the results of one's contemplations than merely to contemplate (IIa IIae, q. 188, a. 6). "Your ways, O Lord, make known to me; teach me your paths." (Ps. 24:4)

Such a life, however, demands that one's labor become a continuation of one's prayer. This does not merely mean an apostolic life based on prayer or the passing on to one's neighbor of the "lights received in prayer"; but, to use the phrases of St. Ignatius, it is contemplation which makes us love creatures in God and God in creatures. In effect, this demands that the hospital nun see Christ in her patients *and* her fellow workers, the nurses and doctors. It means that the teacher must see and find Christ in the students *and* the administrators!

Contemplation must penetrate our whole apostolic life. In that active life it consists in seeing God everywhere, in all the needs of the neighbor whom we serve and educate. Charity toward the neighbor comes from charity toward God. "Thou shalt love the Lord thy God with thy whole heart and with thy whole soul and with thy whole strength and with thy whole mind; *and thy neighbor as thyself.*" (Luke 10:27)

Then too from prayer the worker in the Lord's vineyard draws help to deal with the neighbor *successfully*. Through prayer one purifies one's own soul and obtains a real knowledge of the virtues which are to be taught both by word and example. St. Ignatius, in his *Constitutions,* remarks:

> The means which unite the instrument to God, making him docile in the divine hands, are uprightness, virtue, especially charity, a pure intention of serving God, familiarity with God in prayer, a sincere zeal that aims only at the glory of the Creator and Redeemer of souls, virtues which are more efficacious for good than merely human talents . . .[1]

Have I thus understood my own prayer life, or have I allowed myself at times to set up a kind of departmentalized type of prayer life which never flows over into the apostolic activity which I am supposed by my Rule and way of life to

[1] Quoted from the translation in Brou, *op. cit.,* p. 30.

accomplish? This is a mistaken attitude which I ask God that I may avoid: "My eyes are ever toward the Lord, for he will free my feet from the snare. Look toward me, and have pity on me, for I am alone and afflicted. Relieve the troubles of my heart, and bring me out of my distress" (Ps. 24:15).

Ask earnestly that you may understand the close relationship between your prayer life and your apostolic work of teaching and administration. "Your ways, O Lord, make known to me; teach me your paths, guide me in your truth and teach me, for you are God my savior, and for you I wait all the day." (Ps. 24:4)

19

My Prayer and My Apostolate

1st Prelude: Picture to yourself our Lord as he goes about Palestine teaching and preaching to the people.

2nd Prelude: Ask earnestly for the grace to understand clearly the close relationship between your prayer and your apostolic work.

The spiritual life and prayer of a religious must be fitted to the apostolic vocation. It must promote that vocation. If it must, it can! It is true that there is the danger of giving oneself so much to external activity that the interior life suffers. Writers on prayer, especially if they themselves are members of a contemplative order, have stressed this danger. On the other hand, they have not always appreciated the fact that for those whose apostolate lies directly in work for the neighbor, this very apostolic activity should deepen, not weaken, their prayer life. The hearing of confessions, the distribution of communion, the preaching of sermons, the teaching of classes, the counselling of students—all these should react upon the interior life of good religious to strengthen and increase their virtues of faith, hope and charity. "Your ways, O Lord, make known to me; teach me your paths." (Ps. 24:4)

Very often the amount of self-denial that has to go into the preparation and teaching of a series of classes is completely overlooked by writers unfamiliar with this apostolate. The amount of patience needed in administration is unknown only to those who have never had such positions. Student counsellors are constantly called upon to give of their time and energy when very often that is the last thing they desire. Homework and its correction is often much more of a burden to the teacher than the pupil. These and a score of other opportunities for self-denial and the real practice of charity are always before us.

The apostolic life in itself is a school of virtue, and if we have not succeeded in advancing in virtue, it is very probably because we have not done *our* homework. There is no surer or safer way to make spiritual progress than through self-denial, and the apostolic life of teaching and administration is full of opportunities for this. "Guide me in your truth and teach me, for you are God my savior, and for you I wait all the day." (Ps. 24:5) "Send forth your light and your fidelity; they shall lead me on and bring me to your holy mountain, to your dwelling-place." (Ps. 42:3)

Let me carefully examine my attitudes toward my apostolic work of teaching or administration. Do I consistently strive to see God in creatures, in my pupils and students, in those with whom I work? If I use a preparatory prayer at class time, what are the intentions I have? In the oral prayers I say during the day, do I pray for a successful apostolate in my teaching and administration? Have I *consistently* used the exercises of the examination of conscience, especially the particular examination, to make myself a more ready instrument in the hands of God for my apostolic work? Does my prayer life effectively and constantly promote my apostolic life? I can ask myself these and a score of other questions. And I probably should.

In thanksgiving for my vocation let me say prayerfully Psalm 9. "I will give thanks to you, O Lord, with all my heart; I will declare all your wondrous deeds. I will be glad and exult in you; I will sing praise to your name, Most High . . ."

20

The Value of Teaching

1st Prelude: Imagine yourself sitting in the front row of a group listening to our Lord's teaching.

2nd Prelude: The grace to understand the value of your work as a teacher or administrator.

One of the quickest ways to understand the value of teaching, whether it be in the primary school or the graduate seminar, is to consider the amount of money spent upon this branch of human endeavor by the various nations of the world. Especially is this true in the United States where hundreds of millions of dollars are spent annually on the education of American youth. And this is not a phenomenon of the past few years but has gone on year after year for many decades. Nor is there any indication that such huge expenditures will cease; rather the forecast is for continual increase in the educational budget. Each year we are told how necessary it is to spend more and more.

The reason for this is that education forms the youth of a land, and teachers give the education. We are learning too at great cost that an educational system which leaves out religious training cannot hope to succeed.

In my case do I realize fully the great opportunities for good that I as a teacher or educational administrator have at hand? Do I often pray for success in my classes? Do I remember my pupils in my Masses and Holy Communions? How often have I thanked God for the great grace of my vocation in the educational world?

Another short cut to an understanding of the value of the educational apostolate is to consider the tactics of the enemy. Note how every godless dictator of the present century has tried to snatch Christian youth away from the Church. How much time, how much money have they spent in forming their own schools, in training youth in their own anti-Christian systems! Look at the work of the Communist leaders today in all the lands they have thus far captured. Control, absolute control of education is their primary objective, and for this they are willing and glad to spend untold efforts. Communist educators and their schools strive to inculcate the Communist "virtues"—love of country, hatred for the "enemies," obedience to authority, love of work and the labor discipline, and conformity of the individual to the state. One official manual of Communist education puts their objective thus: "To instill into the minds of the younger generation, the ideology of Communism and to shape Marxist-Leninist world outlook, to inculcate a spirit of Soviet patriotism and Bolshevik ideas."

What is my own appreciation of my work and duties as a teacher or administrator in my school? Do I fully understand the tremendous importance of a truly religious and

Christian education? Am I training my pupils as effectively
in the Christian tradition as my opposite number is training
future Communists? In my case are the children of light far
behind the children of darkness?

The long history of Christianity shows clearly that the
conversion of individuals and whole peoples to Christianity has been a result of Christian education. From the
monastic and cathedral schools to the medieval univer-
sities, from the Renaissance colleges to the vast networks of
schools in the modern period, the Christian teacher has always been in the vanguard of the apostolate. What is the
crying need of the missions today—schools!

The work of Christ's enemies, their constant attempts to
destroy Christian school systems should teach me the value
of my own work as an educator, as one who forms the
future Christian generation. How often have I thanked God
during the past month for the great privilege of being a
teacher or administrator, having a part in the formation of
Catholic youth? Let me say slowly and prayerfully Psalm
115: ". . . How shall I make a return to the Lord for all the
good he has done for me? . . . My vows to the Lord I will
pay . . . O Lord, I am your servant; . . . To you will I offer
sacrifice of thanksgiving . . ."

21

The Pupils of Our Lord

1st Prelude: Look around carefully at the groups of people who have come to hear Christ teaching.

2nd Prelude: Ask earnestly for the grace you want from this meditation, namely, the grace of imitating Christ the Teacher.

Sometimes we forget that the chief work of our Lord was teaching. For some years he conducted a series of lectures, and more especially, with regard to a small group of followers, a true school. Let us consider the various types of people whom our Lord had as students and "disciples."

First of all, the average person to whom he preached was for the most part a relatively poor peasant, self-opinionated, conservative, knowing his own mind. Some of them were interested, many of them were merely curious. They came to hear what this new preacher had to say and to watch his power of miracles which fascinated them. Yet how few really profited from his teaching.

We might apply this to our own experiences in the classroom. If at times we feel discouraged with the result of our efforts, we can recall the difficulties under which our Lord had to conduct his classes. Without the fine rooms of those teaching in the Temple, he was at the mercy of wind and weather!

A second group of listeners should not be forgotten— these are the pharisees and the doctors of law. Now and then the gospel tells us of their presence at our Lord's discourses, and always they formed a *critical and hostile* audience. They came not so much to listen as to criticize. Sometimes they made their criticism vocal; they even considered him a blasphemer. When our Lord cured "a possessed man who was blind and dumb," the crowd was amazed; the pharisees only said, "This man does not cast out devils except by Beelzebub, the prince of devils" (Matt. 12:24).

At times when we have pupils who seem to be more anxious to put clever questions than to learn the matter at hand, we might well remember our Lord's problems. And we can examine our conscience upon our attitude toward our students, especially when they seem to be attempting to "ensnare us in our speech." Do we treat them kindly or sarcastically? How much have we learned from Christ about the true qualities needed in a good teacher?

The third group of listeners was composed of the disciples and the Twelve Apostles selected by our Lord himself. And yet even with these students, how often he found difficulties! They too were men of their times. They had expected a great political and religious leader who would free Israel from the hated Romans. Even after his long teaching and training, just before the Ascension, Christ was asked

the question: "Lord wilt thou at this time restore the kingdom to Israel?" (Acts 1:6). At times the gospel shows the
group bickering among themselves about first places at
table; one of these quarrels occurred even at the Last Supper. "Now there arose also a dispute among them which of
them was reputed to be the greatest." (Luke 22:24)

The Apostles whom our Lord selected were not well-
educated men, but average peasants and fishermen, certainly not in the class of the scribes and pharisees. They had
strong prejudices and antipathies, as was evident when the
Samaritan townsfolk refused entrance to the group on their
way to Jerusalem. John and James thereupon asked, "Lord,
wilt thou that we bid fire come down from heaven and
consume them?" and our Lord "turned and rebuked them"
(Luke 9:54).

Such were the men whom our Lord trained to be his
Apostles and to whom he gave great powers. As we watch
him carefully and patiently educating these Galileans, let us
examine our own attitudes as teachers or administrators
toward the students and people with whom we have to deal.
How much more respectful they are than the average audience he had! How much more sincere than the pharisees! In
general, especially if we are teaching high school or college
students, how much better-educated and prepared are our
students than the ones our Lord had in his classes. Yet
how often have we lost patience with our students and perhaps in a few harsh and bitter words destroyed the work of
weeks?

Let me say slowly and confidently Psalm 39.

I have waited, waited for the Lord, and he stooped toward me and heard my cry. He drew me out of the pit
of destruction, out of the mud of the swamp; He set
my feet upon a crag; he made firm my steps. And he
put a new song into my mouth, a hymn to our God . . .
To do your will, O my God, is my delight, and your
law is within my heart! . . .

22

Characteristics of a Good Teacher:
Approachableness

1st Prelude: Observe our Lord surrounded by a crowd of eager, jostling peasant farmers in the streets of Capharnaum.

2nd Prelude: Beg for the grace you want today—to imitate Christ the Teacher.

One characteristic essential to a good teacher is an ability to treat and meet students easily, constantly. The good teacher has to be *approachable*. Otherwise his or her efforts will lose a great deal of their effectiveness. If the pupils fear their teacher, if they find their teacher distant, difficult to approach, one who "never has any time for them," they will also find it difficult to learn from that teacher. Such teachers will have little real influence in the formation of the intellectual and moral character of their pupils and students; in other words, such teachers will not really teach effectively.

For our own improvement as teachers, let us recall the approachableness of Christ the Teacher. His very birth at

Bethlehem signaled clearly what was to be. He was born in a
cave, a cavern for animals in the hillside. There are no
doors on a cave; we do not expect a butler to come to the
entrance and ask for our card. We just walk right in. And
throughout his life Christ continued to be easy to speak
with and easy to reach whenever men wanted to come to
him. His trade as a carpenter made him the handyman of
Nazareth and at the beck and call of everyone in the village. He made the very ordinary things for everyday use,
and his work made his shop a place where ordinary people
came and went with considerable frequency.

When we observe him during his public life, how often
do we see him burdened with the cares of others, constantly
helping them, answering their questions, spurring on their
flagging interest. Our Lord was in the midst of a most serious instruction, in front of the pharisees and learned men of
his culture, yet he had an immediate eye of pity for the poor
cripple lowered from the roof of the crowded room and
placed at his feet (Luke 5:18). To the poor or to the rich,
he was equally approachable. He had time for the learned
Nicodemus and for the ignorant Galilean peasants. Christ
the Teacher was constantly approachable.

Let me compare my conduct with his example. Can my
students consult me easily and frequently or do I set up a
wall around myself? Am I willing to interrupt my work,
sometimes on a very busy day, to see a pupil for counselling
and help? When I am in the midst of a fine periodic sentence in my patiently-prepared lecture and the hand of the

slowest pupil starts waving in front of me, how do I react? Class discipline must be had, but the good teacher never allows it to become an obstacle to effective teaching.

It is very difficult to be able to exercise this approachableness of our Lord constantly and consistently. It requires a high degree of self-sacrifice and self-control which will be gained only by much prayer and constant vigilance. But the influence of such a teacher upon the student body and the school in general is very great indeed. It may be some casual conversation which starts the whole development of a vocation; some ordinary question which opens up to a student a whole vista of good to be done. A book recommended, an article cited—these can change a life! But it is the approachable teacher who succeeds in making the recommendation. It is the teacher who has an interest in the students and their problems, in their ambitions and plans to whom they like to go and with whom they prefer to speak.

What have I done to acquire and increase this characteristic in my apostolate of teaching? What shall I do about it *today?*

23

Characteristics of a Good Teacher:
Patience

1st Prelude: Note our Lord's patience toward those he is teaching.

2nd Prelude: To ask earnestly for the grace of patience.

Perhaps the most necessary virtue of a good teacher is patience! All educators need patience; this is true of the primary school teacher as well as those teaching in high school or college. Sometimes it is the temperament of a certain student, perhaps even of a whole class which seems to set us on edge as soon as we walk into the classroom. Sometimes it is the wearying task of repeating, time after time, truths which seem so clear to us that we cannot understand how our students miss them. Sometimes it is a student in whom we had put great hope and with whom we had spent a great deal of time whose final record proves a great disappointment to us. Correcting papers, red-penciling the same absurdities day after weary day demands a great deal of patience. Every teacher could add a score of other opportunities for the practice of this great teaching virtue.

Patience has been defined as a Christian virtue which enables us to withstand with "equanimity of soul" and for the love of our Lord, all physical and moral sufferings. We all know that there are many kinds of suffering in our lives which, if only we accepted them in the right spirit, could make us very holy people. But often enough it is with bitterness rather than resignation that we meet the daily problems that beset us. And sometimes when we do endure them, it is rather out of pride and with tight lips that we do so. We must teach ourselves to recognize in such difficulties the will of God and to bear up under them, motivated by the thought of Christ who suffered and died for each of us. Each day we say the Morning Offering in which we offer clearly the sufferings of that day, but when the early morning classes come, or our round of administrative duties begins to overwhelm us, this seems to slip our mind.

Our Lord's patient enduring of the ignorance and misunderstanding which he constantly had to face should be a powerful stimulus to us in our work. Very often his pupils were refractory, sometimes they tried to trip him in his speech, and even the best of them frequently misunderstood his meaning. Yet Christ never lost patience with his hearers despite their inattention, their prejudices, or their criticism of his explanations.

As we study the life of Christ, our purpose is to try to make ourselves more like him in all our actions, especially in our teaching or administrative work. We want to become truly Christ-like, Christians in the full sense of the word.

For this purpose our motive in accepting a difficulty should
be to become more like our Divine Model, whether that
difficulty be a sudden (and to us disastrous) change of
schedule or a class that seems to have built-in obstacles to
learning.

With this purpose in mind, let me review the usual
actions and duties of my day and note where opportunities
for the practice of patience and therefore growth in the
supernatural life may have escaped me. It might pay me to
check my schedule carefully, hour by hour, person by person, duty by duty, just to see in what areas of my life great
opportunities may be slipping by unheeded. When I have
made this review, carefully and completely, let me ask
myself—what shall I do about this *today*.

Let me say as well as I can Psalm 30: "In you, O Lord, I
take refuge; let me never be put to shame. In your justice
rescue me, incline your ear to me, make haste to deliver
me! . . . Have pity on me, O Lord, for I am in distress. . . .
But my trust is in you, O Lord . . ."

24

Characteristics of a Good Teacher: Class Preparation

1st Prelude: Listen carefully to our Lord as he tells the story of the Good Samaritan.

2nd Prelude: Ask for the grace you want from this meditation: to become a better and more Christ-like teacher.

Sometimes in the busy life of a teacher, there seems so little time to prepare classes. And sometimes this may not strike us as anything that we should be troubled about. But maybe it should trouble us! A teacher must have knowledge to impart. Without knowledge to teach, what is a teacher but a "tinkling cymbal"? Even those who have taught the same matter several times know that without preparation their classes are far from perfect. Instead of taking the pupils through a graded series of classes which will end in a mastery, according to the pupils' ability and energy, of a certain area of knowledge, their classes are a series of jerky starts and stops, with relatively little if any progress being made from day to day.

Perhaps I should examine my attitude toward my own

classes. If I am a teacher, much of my religious life is spent in this function. If I fail as a teacher, how can I possibly expect to make progress in my religious life when teaching forms so great a part of it? This is my apostolate; if it is unsuccessfully and inefficiently done, a chief instrument of my perfection is missed. Let me consider carefully my own attitudes toward my classes. Do I devote time to a careful preparation of them; do I do the necessary reading? Are my class notes in order, or are they an intellectual labyrinth? Have I kept up my education? Have I read at least one article in the past month to help my teaching and store of knowledge? If I have found that too many things have been given to me to do outside of my teaching, have I carefully explained this to the correct superiors—or have I just griped to others?

I might look too at the way in which I present the knowledge I have gained. It is not only a matter of preparing clear presentations of the matter to be taught, of outlines adequately developed; it is also a question of attitude. In solving a student's difficulties, in answering the pupils' questions, do I make use of my superior knowledge as a teacher in a way which aids but does not antagonize the student? Are my answers not only clear, but honest? If the question opens up a new difficulty for *me,* do I admit it, or do I take refuge in generalities, beating about the intellectual bush?

The example of our Lord in answering the question of "a certain lawyer who got up to test him" (Luke 10:25 ff.) teaches me. Our Lord drew the correct answer from him and then commended him upon it. But the lawyer, "wishing to justify himself" and not let it appear that his question was after all such a simple one, went on to ask, "And who is my neighbor?" Despite the evident attempt to put him upon the spot, note the wonderful answer which our Lord gave. At the end he once more asked the man a key question: "Which of these three, in thy opinion, proved himself neighbor to him who fell among the robbers?" Even then the man apparently found it too difficult to use the word "Samaritan," and so his answer was, "He who took pity on him." And in return he received our Lord's advice, "Go and do thou also in like manner."

Let me read that event over several times so that I may apply it to my own teaching. Let me examine myself in regard to my own conduct when it seems that my students are "getting up to test me."

25

The Value of Obedience

1st Prelude: Picture to yourself our Lord saying personally to you: "If you love me, keep my commandments" (John 15:10).

2nd Prelude: To ask God earnestly and sincerely for the grace to become more obedient each day.

It is sometimes said that members of religious orders and congregations are scarcely ever commanded to do anything explicitly in virtue of obedience. At first glance this would seem to indicate that the vow of obedience has little influence on our religious lives. A second glance and a few years of experience in any religious institute will give multiple proof to the contrary.

Obedience enters into every activity and corner of our religious lives. Whether we are going to our classes or to our office, whether we are on our way to say our prayers or to eat our dinner, whether we are getting up in the morning or going to bed at night, we are following a schedule. And we ourselves did not make up that schedule. (How well we know it!) All the livelong day we are obeying and conforming ourselves to some aspect of the scheduled plan which has been placed before us as our part in the service of the Lord.

Still, though obedience permeates our life generally, it can sometimes happen that the routine of an office or teaching position makes us forget this fact—that is, until a directive from our superior awakens us to the realization that obedience enters into this facet of our lives as well. But we can grow so used to things that we may forget that obedience forms so essential a part of our religious lives. We tend to forget the value of this great virtue which the Fathers of the Church and the founders of religious institutes praised so highly. Why they praised it so highly is clear enough—without it the organization of which we are members would disintegrate.

But to keep the spotlight on ourselves, the value comes from what we offer to God in obedience: not money or valued external possessions, but something much more difficult to give up—ourselves. The "obedient man is made a living holocaust," an offering given entirely to God with nothing taken back. Such a one keeps nothing back from God, no, not even his own will. And we all know that this is the part of ourselves that we most want to hang on to. In obedience we give ourselves completely to God through the hands of our superiors—this is what we agreed to when we made our vows. Our talents, our good qualities, our ambitions and desires, all these we turned over to him entirely. This is the great value of our obedience; we have no greater gift to give to our Lord than ourselves.

Let me quietly talk over this very important matter with

the Master. How many years now have I been in obedience? How well have I been living up to this promise? Are there nooks and crannies in my everyday life where I do not allow him to come? Or can I honestly say that everything I do, that all my daily activity is part and parcel of my obedience? This does not mean that obedience has become easier for me. But even if it has I should not measure the value of things by the ease with which I do them. For some, obedience seems to grow more difficult with the passing years, but this may merely mean that our Lord is letting them prove their love more clearly. At any rate, every now and then it is a good thing for me to think about my practice of obedience, since it is so essential to his service.

Let me slowly go over the prayer known as the *Suscipe* and see how it applies to the various things I did yesterday, the things I intend to do today for his service.

Take, O Lord, and receive all my liberty, my memory, my understanding, and my entire will. Whatever I have or hold, Thou has given me; I restore it all to Thee and surrender it wholly to be governed by Thy will. Give me only Thy love and Thy grace, and I am rich enough and ask for nothing more.

26

The Perfection of Obedience

1st Prelude: Recall our Lord's words: "If you love me, keep my commandments" (John 15:10).

2nd Prelude: The grace to mirror in your life the obedience of Christ.

When we think of obedience we usually tend to think of it in terms of military obedience. We recall the difficult commands which have been carried out by soldiers, the courage required to advance under fire. We think too of the promptness required in execution of the command. Yet when we come to consider religious obedience carefully, we find that this is not enough. In fact, St. Ignatius, when writing his classic letter on obedience, pointed out that the mere execution of what is commanded is only the first degree of obedience. ". . . It does not deserve the name unless it attain the merit of obedience by rising to the second degree, which is to make the Superior's will one's own, so that there will be not merely the effective fulfilling of the command, but an interior conformity in that both wish and do not wish the same." The saints exhort us to offer freely our will to our Lord through his ministers. By so doing we really restore our will, our most precious possession, to God by means of our obedience.

The saints also warn us not to attempt to draw the will of the Superior to our own, which would be in effect making God do our will instead of our doing his. There are many ways of deceiving ourselves in this matter. Perhaps I should pause here and ask myself honestly whether there are areas in my life where I am not doing the Superior's will but rather the Superior is doing my will.

There is a higher degree still than the obedience of the will, and that is the obedience of the understanding. This means that a person in religious life should "not only wish the same as the Superior, but think the same, submitting his own judgment to the Superior's, so far as a devout will can incline the understanding." We all know that our will and inclinations affect our judgment and our opinions; we naturally tend to think highly of our school, our team, our house. And we know, too, that many times when we are not sure about the truth our will and inclinations push us to favor one side rather than another. The same thing can happen in matters of obedience. Usually we do not know all the facts nor all the alternatives, and consequently the truth of the matter is not perfectly clear to us. In such cases our will should incline us to bring our judgment into conformity with that of our Superior.

This is what is meant when one says that obedience is a "holocaust"; the whole person, "without the slightest reserve, is offered in the fire of charity to his Creator and Lord." It is a complete surrender of ourselves into the hands of Divine Providence. It is not an easy gift to make to God, but it is a very great one. Most of us will admit that we ourselves do not always know what is best for us. And so to keep our will and understanding from going astray, we conform it to the will of God as expressed to us through our Superiors.

This doctrine is not news to me! I have thought about it many times during my religious life. Since it involves the greatest perfection, let me pass in review the various details of my present life in religion and see how obedience enters into them. Am I practicing at least the second degree of obedience by conforming my will and my wishes to those of God as made evident to me through my Superiors? How often do I strive to practice the highest obedience, that of my understanding, by trying to think the same as my Superiors?

In my colloquies during this meditation let me go over this prayer again and again.

Take, O Lord, and receive all my liberty, my memory, my understanding, and my entire will. Whatever I have or hold, Thou has given me; I restore it all to Thee and surrender it wholly to be governed by Thy will. Give me only Thy love and Thy grace, and I am rich enough and ask for nothing more.

27

Means of Achieving Obedience

1st Prelude: Imagine yourself present at the Last Supper as our Lord says to the Apostles: "If you love me, keep my commandments" (John 15:10).

2nd Prelude: To beg for what you want from this morning's prayer—the grace to increase in the virtue of obedience.

We admit to ourselves the value of religious obedience, we know too that it forms the very essence of our religious life. But how often have we thought about the means to achieve it? We have read them in our spiritual reading, but how often have we pondered over them?

First of all, there is the general advice that if we are humble and meek of heart, we will find obedience easy to practice. In addition to these general means, however, there are some special ones that it might be well for me to think about. For instance, do I behold in my Superior, not someone weak, ignorant and subject to error, but "rather Him whom you obey, Christ, the highest Wisdom, immeasurable Goodness and infinite Charity, who you know cannot be deceived and will not deceive you"?

The Superior is to be obeyed, not because he or she is prudent or good or qualified by any other of God's gifts, but because such a one holds God's place and authority, as Eternal Truth has said, "He who hears you, hears me; he who rejects you, rejects me." I should wish, therefore, that all of you would train yourselves to recognize Christ our Lord in any Superior whomsoever, and with all devotion to reverence and obey the Divine Majesty in him.

These quotations from St. Ignatius' classic letter on obedience are merely the summary of centuries of monastic practice and advice in regard to this fundamental virtue. We do not obey our Superiors because they are "prudent or good or qualified by any other of God's gifts": we obey them because they "hold the place of God." When the Superior commands we "do not take his voice to be any other than the voice of Christ."

A second means to help ourselves to perfect obedience is to habitually and quickly look for reasons to defend the commands of Superiors rather than to disapprove of them. This takes practice and lots of it. The point is that if we develop this optimistic attitude our obedience becomes easier and we go along cheerfully and calmly. As Pope St. Leo remarked, "It is not hard to serve when we love what is commanded."

Let me carefully think over these two means and my general attitude toward the commands and regulations which come to me in my religious life. Do I find myself calmly and peacefully accepting the yoke of obedience? If not, why not? If I look back into past years and find much more peace of mind at some earlier time, let me carefully examine my attitude toward obedience and my practice of it at that time. The results may surprise me!

In my colloquies during this meditation let me beg for a greater love and esteem of the obedience of our Lord. Recall his words and his deeds.

And He went down with them and came to Nazareth and was subject to them . . . (Luke 2:51) My food is to do the will of Him who sent me, to accomplish His work. (John 4:34) For I have come down from heaven, not to do my own will, but the will of Him who sent me. (John 6:38) If you keep my commandments you will abide in my love, as I also have kept my Father's commandments, and abide in His love. (John 15:10)

28

The Peace of Obedience

1st Prelude: Listen carefully to St. Paul saying to you the words he wrote in his Epistle to the Hebrews: "Obey your superiors and be subject to them, for they keep watch as having to render an account of your souls; so that they may do this with joy, and not with grief, for that would not be expedient for you" (Heb. 13:17).

2nd Prelude: Let me ask earnestly for the grace to enjoy the *peace* of obedience.

Most of us have felt at some time that we would be much more successful in doing this or that other type of work. We have been so sure that if we were in another occupation, if we had that other job, we would be doing more for God, achieving more for the Church; in general, we would be more apostolic. This thought can certainly come to everyone in education. There occurs the same routine of classes, the same stupid mistakes, the same regular cycle semester in and semester out; then we pick up the paper and the headlines shout that some part of the world is crashing down, and we feel that we are doing so little about it. We seem to just sit at our desks solving the same "insoluble" problems that came up last year! It all seems so futile at times. We wonder what we got ourselves into.

About this time we should begin to let the peace that comes from obedience sink into our souls. All we have to do is remember the little question and answer we were taught so many years ago as children. We were asked, "Why did God make you?" And we rattled off, "He made me to know him, to love him, to serve him, and to be happy with him forever. . . ." The answer was true, one of the truest things we ever learned. And this service and love consists not of fine and flowery words but of deeds—deeds that often seem humdrum and so ordinary. They consist in finding and doing what he wants us to do.

The finding of God's will is not difficult. It comes to us through the directions of our Superiors, whether that direction happens to have come in this morning's mail or that of twenty years' ago. Knowing his will and his wishes, we pray each day that we may accomplish them. There is no greater possible glory we can give to God. So then let us sit back and relax in the joy of knowing that we are doing just what he wants us to do. This is why we came to religion, this is why we stayed here. This is why we are here now. Those humdrum things which we do each morning and afternoon are not ordinary at all; they are extremely important because they are what he wishes us to do. Our problem is to do them as perfectly as we can. We have found his will; it is there before us. Let us get going and accomplish it!

When I am praying during the colloquies of this meditation let me say the Our Father slowly—very slowly. Let me
dwell especially on those petitions which our Lord taught us
to ask: "Thy Kingdom come, Thy will be done on earth as
it is in Heaven. . . ."

29

The Obedience of St. Joseph

1st Prelude: ". . . Behold, an angel of the Lord appeared
in a dream to Joseph, saying, 'Arise, and take the child and
his mother and flee into Egypt, and remain there until I tell
thee' . . ." (Matt. 2:13)

2nd Prelude: Beg earnestly of St. Joseph to ask our Lord to
give you the grace of obedience.

When we are looking about for an example of a truly
obedient man, we can scarcely do better than think about St.
Joseph. We do not know very much about him except that
he was obedient, and that he obeyed under difficult circumstances. Mary was in the last stages of her pregnancy when
the order came from a pagan government to make a long
and difficult trip so that the tax collectors and census takers
could have more data. Certainly Joseph would seem to have
had a good reason for complaining or at least for postpon-
ing obedience. "And Joseph also went from Galilee out of
the town of Nazareth into Judea to the town of David, which
is called Bethlehem—because he was of the house and family
of David—to register together with Mary his espoused wife,
who was with child." (Luke 2:4)

If things were not difficult enough already, soon after the birth of our Lord, Joseph was told to pack up immediately and flee across the border into safer territory. And the *immediately* meant just that. Joseph did what he was told. ". . . Behold, an angel of the Lord appeared in a dream to Joseph, saying, 'Arise, and take the child and his mother, and flee into Egypt, and remain there until I tell thee. For Herod will seek the child to destroy him.' So he arose, and took the child and his mother by night, and withdrew into Egypt, and remained there until the death of Herod." (Matt. 2:13)

Not only was the obedience of St. Joseph prompt but it was unquestioning. A person with less faith and love might have suggested to the angel that *he* take care of Herod! Or he might have proposed departure to a nearby but obscure town within his own native land; but Egypt! St. Joseph does none of these things. He simply obeys.

Since obedience is so clearly the touchstone of our service to our Lord, let us calmly compare our ordinary attitudes in following the directions from Superiors with the prompt actions of St. Joseph. It will pay me to go over my day, perhaps my week, and see how things go with my own obedience. And in my colloquies during the meditation I can beg St. Joseph for the grace to see things the way he saw them. My difficulties are probably very much smaller than the ones he was faced with; nevertheless, they look like pretty big ones to me. Let me make acts of faith and love so that my own obedience will become more and more like his.

Sometimes when I am sent to a new place to do God's will, it seems that I am truly going into Egypt. Then is the time to remember the example of St. Joseph and pray to him for help. But sometimes due to a change of occupation, or new directives, although I have not gone into Egypt, it seems that Egypt has come to me! Here again the example of St. Joseph should help me to understand that everything is part of God's plan for my sanctification. Naturally, I like the "Yes" Superiors, but the "No" Superiors are part of his plan as well, and sometimes they are very needful to me.

By way of the colloquy at the end of meditation, as well as for those during it, I might well glance at some of the sentiments of Psalm 118, the long psalm praising the law of the Lord.

Happy are they whose way is blameless, who walk in the law of the Lord. Happy are they who observe his decrees, who seek him with all their heart, and do no wrong, but walk in his ways . . . I will keep your statutes; do not utterly forsake me. . . . With all my heart I seek you; let me not stray from your commands. . . .

30

What St. Joseph Did

1st Prelude: Picture to yourself St. Joseph working in his small shop, the front part of his humble home situated on one of the hilly streets of Nazareth.

2nd Prelude: Beg for the grace to always do what God wants you to do.

When we consider the work which St. Joseph did we are brought up rather short. It doesn't fit in with modern ideas of a great work. We are used to the evaluations of the press, of television, of radio: summit conferences, talks about some great national or international problem, striking success in space exploration, new discoveries in the world of medicine! Hammering nails into a few boards doesn't seem very important in comparison. Working on plow handles and repairing furniture in a small hill town in a despised part of the great Roman world empire seems insignificant. But this is not the way God evaluated St. Joseph's work, and God's evaluation is the only one that counts. It will count forever.

The work which St. Joseph did—and he did it all his life long—was very ordinary, very humdrum we would say. He

worked in a small town whose inhabitants, from their reputation, were not very gracious or important. We recall the
scornful words of Nathanael to Philip: "Can anything good
come out of Nazareth?" (John 1:46). Yet St. Joseph spent
long years working and sweating away at manual labor in
this place. His was a job which made him more or less a
handyman of the village, one who had to be at the beck and
call of other people. He had to be pleasant and courteous
under trying circumstances, polite and gracious to ungra-
cious and ungrateful customers. He had to keep his patience
with people who wanted the best work at the cheapest
price.

Against this background of a life spent in manual labor
and poverty, let us place our own type of work. Sometimes
we may be tempted to think that it is not only very ordinary, but perhaps useless; we feel that it doesn't seem to be
the kind of thing that wins souls to God, it doesn't seem
very spiritual. It seems that we are spending day after weary
day, teaching the same classes, correcting the same mistakes. Yet what are we really doing? We are spending our
lives in the work of forming Christian character, in making
better citizens of God's kingdom. We spend our lives teaching in and administering grade and high schools, nurses
training schools, and liberal arts colleges, from which come
graduates not only learned in their specialty and with the
knowledge needful for this world, but ready and able to
lead a life that will bring them to eternal happiness. This is
humdrum? This is useless?

How can we possibly become so mistaken? Because we have let our vision be blurred by really worldly ideals so that the practical effect of our faith is lost upon us. Our faith shows that like St. Joseph we are doing that which God had planned for us from all eternity. We are "doing His will on earth" and we should try to do it "as it is done in Heaven." In the light of God's view of the work of St. Joseph, the foster father of the Redeemer of the World, let us realize the importance of our own work. We are doing *the most important thing we could possibly do* when we carry out God's will. Precisely because the world around us is filled with erroneous views and judgments, because it holds up the false ideals against which Christ warned us, just for these reasons we must beware of its judgments. We must think of things as God thinks of them. We must judge matters as Christ judges them—in the light of eternal values. Then everything snaps into place with a kind of cosmic click. Then *we* have peace. Maybe in my colloquies for this meditation I had better repeat again and again an act of contrition for my blindness.

31

How St. Joseph Did It

1st Prelude: Observe carefully St. Joseph, at times working in his small shop, at other times saying his daily prayers, sometimes conversing with others.

2nd Prelude: Beg the grace to imitate in your small way the manner in which St. Joseph did God's will.

If the work which St. Joseph did during his lifetime was not spectacular or unusual, the *way* he did it was! He fulfilled God's will in a most excellent manner. He showed his love of God in the devotion with which he said his prayers to the praise and reverence of God, in the kindness with which he treated all those with whom he came in contact, in the zeal with which he applied himself to his work. These are the very virtues which are so necessary to each of us in the work which God has given us to do.

We have been told often enough through our reading and spiritual instruction that "we should do well what we do," that in those small everyday affairs of ours lies the perfection of our lives. Yet how little do we really understand this. There are perhaps ten or fifteen different items, work, teaching, recreation, prayers oral and mental, reading, class preparation, and so on that make up my day and my life. It is in these things and the *way* I do them that my perfection is to be found. It is in these matters that I find the will of God in my life. How do I fulfill it?

Perhaps I can take a closer look at this matter. Let me go through the various parts of my day. The many prayers I say—how are they said? The glory which I am supposed to give to God each day—how is this done? The example to others, especially to those of my own community—how well is this given? The many opportunities I have each day to bring God into the lives of others—how do I avail myself of them? Sometimes I think what a wonderful job I would do if I were able to meet more people, have more opportunity to proclaim God's message. Did I ever count up the number of individuals I meet and converse with *every day*—the numbers I meet in my classes, in my administrative work? Just let me do that for a minute or two, and I shall very likely be quite surprised at the total. There are plenty of opportunities in my life, and sometimes by an idea, by a remark, I can change the lives of others to a remarkable degree. Anyone in educational work knows the truth of this.

If I find that I am not succeeding as I wish, let me consider the manner, the *wa*y I am going about doing God's will. On the face of it, St. Joseph probably had far less opportunity than I have of contacting people, of impressing them by word and example. How often have I ever stopped to consider the great opportunities which God gives me

each and every day, the ones he gave me yesterday, the
ones I shall get today? What am I doing with them?

I will give thanks to the Lord with all my heart in
the company and assembly of the just. Great are the
works of the Lord, exquisite in all their delights . . .
The works of his hands are faithful and just . . . His
praise endures forever. (Ps. 110)

32

The Rule: My Portrait of Christ

1st Prelude: Watch our Lord as he goes about a room viewing various portraits of himself.

2nd Prelude: Beg earnestly the grace to form your portrait of Christ correctly.

Let us imagine a room full of pictures of Christ. In one we see him preaching to the crowds on the lakeshore; one shows him healing the sick; one pictures him forgiving the sins of a poor penitent; in another he is praying alone on the mountain; in still another he is working in the carpenter shop at Nazareth. We can imagine our Lord coming into such a room, going from picture to picture, and we can hear him saying, "Yes, this pictures me correctly, and this and this . . ."

Now the founders of the various orders and religious congregations were raised up by God for a very special purpose. They were to form for themselves a portrait of Christ in their own lives. They did so. Moreover, they instituted an organization for others who would work and serve Christ as they had done. In order to make it easier for those who would follow after them, they wrote the Rules or Constitutions of their organization. Thus every founder of a religious order or congregation has drawn a picture of Christ in the rules which he or she set down. It is a specialized portrait which fits their work and their type of service of God. This is the way the members of their organization should form their lives, this is their portrait of Christ. They should make themselves look like that portrait of Christ.

Let us recall to ourselves these important words of Pius XI:

> We exhort all religious to model their lives upon that of their holy Founder who established their order and drew up its constitutions. *In no other way* can they be sure of sharing abundantly in the graces which go with their vocation. Was it not divine inspiration which guided those holy persons in the founding of their institutes. Consequently those members who wish to show forth in their lives that particular characteristic which these wished to be distinctive of their respective congregations do not deviate from the ideals of their founders. . . . Let them carefully obey the laws of their institutes and preserve the manner of life established in the beginning and thus show themselves daily more worthy of the religious state.

And to remind ourselves further of the importance of our rules, let us recall the Code of Canon Law, #593.

Each and every Religious, Superiors as well as subjects, must not only observe faithfully the vows they have pronounced but also live their life in accordance with the Rules and Constitutions of their order *and in this way tend to the perfection of their state* (italics added).

In my colloquies let me pray over this matter carefully. It should give me a great deal of peace of mind to realize the short cut to perfection which God has given me in the Rules and Constitutions of my organization. Have I ever thought much about this? Have I constantly thanked God for this great favor done to *me?* How is my portrait of Christ coming?

Let me recite several times during this meditation the great prayer, *Anima Christi.*

> Soul of Christ, sanctify me.
> Body of Christ, save me.
> Blood of Christ, inebriate me.
> Water from the side of Christ, wash me.
> Passion of Christ, strengthen me.
> O good Jesus, hear me.
> Within Thy wounds hide me.
> Permit me not to be separated from Thee.
> From the wicked foe defend me.
> At the hour of my death call me.
> And bid me come to Thee.
> That with Thy saints I may praise Thee
> For ever and ever. Amen.

33

My Rule of Life

1st Prelude: Picture to yourself our Lord looking at the portrait of himself as sketched in the Rule you follow.

2nd Prelude: Beg fervently for the great grace of keeping your Rule.

Usually the grace we hope to get from our daily meditation is that of knowing, loving, and imitating Christ more and more in our lives. And this is precisely what our Rule helps us to do. For us it is a safe and sure guide to religious perfection. So when we are praying for a better knowledge of Christ and a greater imitation of him in our everyday life, we should connect up this petition with our Rule.

But it is not only in this way that we should think of our Rule; we should remember that it is also the great protection and defense of our organization. The particular spirit and character which singles out our order or congregation derives its full spirit from the Rule and Constitution. Our Rule is our guard. We might compare it to a great system of fortifications planned by a military expert to defend and protect his country. In somewhat the same way the religious founder with a special ideal and objective in mind, pondered, meditated, and carefully wrote the Rule. Just as no two fortresses are exactly alike but must adapt their construction to their objective and to their surroundings, so too, the religious founder has laid special emphasis upon a specific aspect of religious life, the better to ensure the objective of the organization and the perfection of the individual member. Thus we cannot pick and choose the parts of the Rule we intend to follow; if we do, we find to our sorrow that we have weakened the whole structure, and laid ourselves open to serious danger.

On the other hand, we must beware of regarding our Rule or Constitution as a series of dry obligations, just a set of "don'ts." Anyone who tends to perfection in a certain field must follow strict rules. Consider the years of careful work which have gone into the success of the professional athletes about whom we read in our newspapers or see on television. Think of the outstanding artists, the singers for example, whose fundamentally great voices had to be developed through long years of extensive, painstaking, dull, daily practice. Often enough, we know from our own teaching or administrative work the perfection of detail that is required to become outstanding in any field. And in each and every case there are rules and regulations to be followed if one wishes to achieve success. Without them it cannot be done.

The same is true of the religious life. And the regulations and maxims which guarantee success in our search for perfection in the spiritual life are to be found in our Rule. Have I ever sat down to consider the importance of my Rule *now* in my ordinary life? Let me go through the various works which I shall do today and note the connection of my Rule with them. Consider the matter of personal relations with those about me, either as colleague or as director. Have I ever thought of the portions of my Rule which would give me success in these matters? The patience, true charity, freedom from my own self-will and self-love which encourage people to consult me, to want to co-operate with me in achieving God's will—these are all to be found in my Rule. But such applications each one can best make for himself or herself. If I have not pondered the meaning my Rule has in my everyday life, let me begin to do so in this meditation, and perhaps continue for many meditations to come!

Let me pray in my colloquies in this meditation with the words of Psalm 15.

Keep me, O God, for in you I take refuge; I say to the Lord, 'My Lord are you. Apart from you I have no good.' . . . O Lord, my allotted portion and my cup, you it is who hold fast my lot. For me the measuring lines have fallen on pleasant sites; fair to me indeed is my inheritance. I bless the Lord who counsels me . . . You will show me the path to life, fullness of joys in your presence, the delights at your right hand for-ever.

34

My Attitude Toward My Rule

1st Prelude: Imagine our Lord looking at the portrait you have made of yourself.

2nd Prelude: Beg earnestly for the grace to form your portrait of Christ correctly and faithfully.

What we have been thinking about has shown us that our Rule is something very positive, not merely a negative set of "don'ts." The Rule is a safe and sure guide for us in the perfection of our spiritual life. As a result of this knowledge, we naturally esteem and value the Rule. The difficulty is that sometimes we tend to identify the Rule only with certain detailed prescriptions which pertain much more to the novitiate than to our ordinary lives; and since we have left the novitiate, we tend to feel that we have also left our Rule behind us. This is a serious mistake. It is absurd to think that the various founders of the religious orders and congregations have meditated, prayed about, and literally sweated out the Rules and Constitutions which form their portrait of Christ, merely for the one or two years of novitiate training.

The Rule has broad and deep spiritual principles which must govern my whole life. They offer me a safe guide in all the duties and opportunities which my life in religion will give me. Whether in administration or teaching, whether in counselling work or in detailed domestic duties, in all these my Rule offers me the answer. Have I been looking for it there?

From such an esteem and evaluation of the Rule, love will naturally follow. This does not mean a sentimental attachment to it; it means a solid love which will show itself in action.

As mature religious we must have long ago realized that true love consists "more in deeds than in words." This we know. But have we thought about this in connection with our attitude toward our Rule? The greatest respect that can be paid to another is imitation! Our Rule is our picture of Christ. As we love him, so we imitate him; by means of the detailed principles and instructions of our Rule, we form our character according to his image. We become Christians in the true sense—persons in whom others can see Christ. Our Rule makes it possible for us to achieve this in our lives, for it is the sketch of the Christ we are to imitate in the order to which he has called us.

Fidelity to the Rule will follow naturally. We admire fidelity in those around us. When we see an aged doctor still making his hospital rounds day after day, when we see an elderly scholar working steadfastly at the long mortifying grind that true scholarship demands, we are moved deeply by such an example. The religious should also develop the same fidelity. As the years pass, one should grow more and more in appreciation of the Rule by which he or she lives. And as this Rule becomes more and more esteemed and loved, so it becomes more and more a part of our character.

Here again the words of our Lord must ever ring in our ears: "If you love me, keep my commandments." In my colloquies during this meditation let me pray for the great grace of fidelity to my Rule.

35

Rewards of the Rule

1st Prelude: Imagine our Lord looking at the portrait of himself as sketched in the Rule you follow.

2nd Prelude: Beg for a deeper supernatural understanding of the value of your Rule.

In thinking about the importance of my Rule in my everyday religious life, I might think and pray about the *rewards* which will come to me from a careful keeping of the Rule. First of all there is the reward of *perfection*. After all, this is what I have vowed to strive for, this is the whole purpose of my life in religion! I could have served God in the world, in the place where I was, but I followed his call because I wanted to follow him more perfectly. I wanted perfection, not just ordinary service, and he gave me this ambition and the grace to follow his call. Just as the great athletes and artists must carefully follow the rules of the game if they are to develop the perfection which they ardently desire, so we religious must follow our Rule if we are seriously striving for perfection in the religious life. The Rule is our short cut to perfection.

Through our Rule we also gain *efficiency* in our super-natural work. Fundamentally, we are striving to make our selves better and to bring others to God. For these objectives we must have God's help and grace. The closer we are to God the more efficient instruments we become for his work. Natural ability is not enough in our job. We have to have supernatural help. "Without Me you can do nothing," said our Lord, and he meant it. Furthermore, in any organization the effort must be corporate. We must work together as a group, and our Rule shows clearly how we can participate in this corporate apostolate.

Finally, we get *peace*. And we know how much we desire that! It is a deep, interior peace which sustains us in the various difficulties which come along, day after day. We know that our work is what God wishes us to do and the Rule points out the way in which we should do his will. This means that what we are doing is the most important thing we could be doing. Our business is to do it as perfectly as we possibly can, and our Rule tells us how this is to be achieved.

Have I ever thought much about this aspect of my Rule? Let me think and pray about these rewards and use as a starting point in my colloquies thoughts such as these from the Bible.

The law of the Lord is perfect, refreshing the soul;
the decree of the Lord is trustworthy, giving wisdom
to the simple. The precepts of the Lord are right, rejoic-

ing the heart; the command of the Lord is clear, en-
lightening the eye. . . . Though your servant is careful
of them, very diligent in keeping them, yet who can
detect failings? Cleanse me from my unknown faults!
From wanton sin especially, restrain your servant; let
it not rule over me. . . . Let the words of my mouth
and the thought of my heart find favor before you. . . .
(Ps. 18)

My son, forget not my teaching, keep in mind my
commands; For many days, and years of life, and
peace, will they bring you. (Prov. 3:1)

If any man love me, he will keep my word, and my
Father will love him, and we will come to him and
make our abode with him. . . . (John 14:23)

36

Growing to Love My Rule of Life

1st Prelude: Picture to yourself your founder carefully writing the Rule and Constitution.

2nd Prelude: Ask earnestly that you may receive the grace to love and follow your Rule of life.

Thinking and praying about our Rule as we have been doing, we are naturally anxious to increase our love and esteem of it. How does one go about this? Well, look at those around us in the world today who are seeking perfection in a certain area. The doctor must read about his subject, his field of specialization, he must learn what is the latest discovery; the lawyer must read his cases and keep abreast of the latest discussions and interpretations of the law. The businessman too reads his professional trade journal. Everybody "keeps up in their field."

So too the religious must know their Rule, read modern explanations or commentaries upon it, familiarize themselves with the modern applications of it. They should read the lives of those who have sanctified themselves through the same Rule or one similar to it, men and women who have become saints in a way of life similar to their own: saints who have sanctified themselves in the classroom or office; scholars and teachers like Cardinal Bellarmine; writers like St. Peter Canisius; administrators like St. Francis Cabrini or St. Ignatius of Loyola.

There are so many saints and so many books about them that we must pick and choose, and we should select *those whose lives bear some relation to our own.* Very likely it would not have helped a Father of the Desert (had he had the opportunity!) to read the life of a religious hospital administrator, and modern religious may not realize that to confine their reading to the lives of saints who followed a Rule completely different from theirs may have *very little formative influence* on their own lives—and this is not good.

Then, of course, there is the subject of my daily meditation. At times why not select one section of my Rule and see how I am applying it to my everyday life? Doubtless there will be many applications which I shall discover for myself. And almost always whatever I discover for myself will have a deeper influence on me than what I am told by others! As I meditate and pray about my Rule, my love for it will increase and become a vivid part of my religious life. The sentiments of Psalm 118 will gradually become my own attitude toward my Rule.

Happy are they whose way is blameless, who walk in the law of the Lord. Happy are they who observe his decrees, who seek him with all their heart, and do no wrong, but walk in his ways. . . . Open my eyes that I may consider the wonders of your law. I am a wayfarer of earth; hide not your commands from me. . . . Yes, your decrees are my delight; they are my counselors. . . . Make me understand the way of your precepts, and I will meditate on your wondrous deeds. My soul weeps for sorrow; strengthen me according to your words. . . . Give me discernment, that I may observe your law and keep it with all my heart. . . .

Thus let me pray slowly this great psalm of the love of God's law and his directions. And his directions are to be found in my Rule.

37

Conversational Opportunities

1st Prelude: Let me imagine myself present as our Lord converses and deals with his Apostles.

2nd Prelude: Beg for the grace to understand the many opportunities which you have to exercise the apostolate of the spoken word.

It has been estimated that there are more than 250 million telephone conversations *every day* in the United States alone! Just think how many *billions* of face-to-face conversations take place throughout the whole world each day! We are astounded at the incredible numbers, and we ought to be equally astounded when we think of the possibilities of good and evil which such conversations afford. How many men and women are turned away from God through such communications! How many perverted to Communism or atheism! On the other hand, how many are spurred on to greater service of God in their lives by a passing word; how many vocations are begun or fostered by a short conversation!

Let us turn the spotlight upon ourselves. Do we not often think of missionaries in foreign lands, picturing to ourselves their life of preaching and advising others in the way of salvation. Perhaps we secretly envy them their opportunities. Do I ever stop to think how many opportunities I have today to influence others, to help them serve God better? Let me just go through my day, hour by hour. How many people, students and colleagues, shall I meet today, either for a brief greeting, or for an extended conversation? Let me count them up one by one. I may be amazed, perhaps even frightened, at the number of people I shall meet today. And this goes on day after day! What effect will my words have upon them? Will they see in me another Christ? Will my hundreds of conversations be an influence for good or for evil in others' lives?

If I add to the number of people I shall meet in my capacity as a teacher or administrator the members of my community with whom I shall deal, or take recreation, or shall merely pass in the corridor—the number becomes larger and larger. Perhaps I shall have fifty or a hundred or two hundred conversations today—some of them of ten seconds, some of them merely a brief answer on the phone, others two or three minutes, others more extended. Every one of these is but another opportunity to exercise the apostolate of the spoken word. What I say, how I say it, my courtesy or lack of it, the understanding way I receive the question or the bark-like answer I may return—all these will be part of my day. All these conversations will be powerful stimulants for good or for evil upon all those around me. This is a frightening thought. Yet I cannot escape it. I do not, I cannot, live in a vacuum! What I do, what I say, how I say it, all these things greatly influence those about me whether I like it or not. These influences are as inexorably present as the laws of nature.

Let me quietly pray about this matter. Perhaps I have never fully realized the vast opportunities afforded me each day to aid in the building of Christ's kingdom. Perhaps I never really considered conversation as a form of the apostolate. Perhaps I never thought about how many chances I have to share my good ideas with others. Let me recall the words of the psalmist: "Let the words of my mouth and the thought of my heart find favor before you, O Lord . . ." (Ps. 18:15); and "Then my tongue shall recount your justice, your praise, all the day" (Ps. 34:28).

38

Conversational Helps

1st Prelude: Let me imagine myself present as our Lord converses with the people who come to see him, for example, Nicodemus (John 3:1 ff.).

2nd Prelude: Beg the grace to make more apostolic use of your conversational opportunities.

There are some persons who have a natural interest and liking for others, and for them conversation tends to come easily and without great effort on their part. Others tend to be self-centered and taken up with their own affairs, and they must train themselves to pay more attention to the interests of others.

Our Lord has said clearly: "By this will men know that you are my disciples, if you have love for one another" (John 13:35). If we love others, it tends to show clearly in our attitudes toward them, and they immediately recognize it when we speak to them and converse with them. They find conversation with us is easy, for they see that we are really interested in their opinions, their plans, their ambitions, and they are thus in a position to be benefited by our conversation with them. Our pupils and students, those who come to consult us, all of these people sense our attitude toward them very quickly. If they feel that we are busy or preoccupied with other things, that we are not interested in them, then our opportunities for influencing them by our conversations are seriously handicapped right from the start.

This interest in others can be shown very simply in our attitude as listeners. Are we good listeners? If we are not, we shall never be good conversationalists. If we find ourselves always monopolizing the talk, if we consistently interrupt others, speaking our own opinions before hearing what the other person has to say, then we can be fairly sure that we are not good conversationalists. A good conversationalist has to be a good listener, for conversation is the opposite of monologue.

Furthermore, a good listener often saves himself or herself serious errors. Perhaps in advising others or in answering what we think are their questions, we have sometimes hastily interrupted them to give our answer (sometimes a lengthy one), only to find that our detailed answer was quite beside the point when the questioner has had a chance to explain the matter more fully. Perhaps we found this experience quite embarrassing! Well, if we had been good listeners it would never have happened. It has been well said that "a good listener is not only popular but after a while he knows something"!

A good conversationalist needs the virtue of charity and that of patience. He must not only have a deep love for others, but he must have the patience to hear them out. If he or she combines these virtues with zeal to benefit others by conversation, to share the truth and the knowledge which is in his or her possession as an experienced teacher or administrator, then there is no doubt that the apostolate of conversation will become a significant part of that person's life.

It will be well for me to think over these matters carefully. In the ordinary course of events a very great number of opportunities to influence others by conversation will be mine. Very often they will come to me whether I seek them or not. Let me ask myself what I have done about these opportunities in the past, in the different positions I have held. What am I going to do about them at the present time? What shall I plan to do about them in the future— *today?*

39

Practice Makes Better Conversations

1st Prelude: Let me imagine myself present as our Lord and his disciples converse with the people who come to see them.

2nd Prelude: Beg for the grace to become more Christ-like in your conversation today.

To become a good conversationalist one must, as in every other good skill or facility which we humans can pick up, practice at it! And in this matter we can imitate the people around us who, from a purely wordly point of view, strive to make their company acceptable to others and to develop and perfect their powers of communication. A few tips might help us.[1]

We might first of all *prepare* ourselves for our daily conversations. The ideas we would like to share with those about us, the truths which we have and which will help those with whom we work and those whom we direct and

[1] *Christopher News Notes* (May, 1964, No. 136) has a summary of "21 Ways to Improve Your Conversation." Write for it (The Christophers, 16 E. 48th St., New York 10017)—it's free!

counsel, instruct and teach—let us think about these ideas and about how we can easily communicate them to others. An interesting and accurate description of conversational techniques is the following: "He who carefully listens, pointedly asks, calmly speaks, coolly answers, and ceases when he has no more to say, is in possession of some of the best requisites of conversation."

Then, too, we should be constructive and cheerful in our conversations. Nobody likes to listen to a perennial griper. We should beware of always finding fault with the things about us. We should also beware of constantly correcting others, especially our pupils or persons who in some way are under our guidance or authority. Rather we should be cheerful and optimistic in our conversations, and if we have a sense of humor and a humorous way of saying things, let us not leave this talent undeveloped.

Let us make each one of our conversations count. We have to talk with many people today whether we like it or not; let us try to get some good points across while we are conversing. A casual comment on the importance of teaching, for instance, has given the inspiration for the beginning of more than one teaching career. Often enough it doesn't require a great deal of effort to turn a rather pointless conversation into a definite and helpful one.

One should not get the idea that such conversations have to be lengthy! We are all busy people. Just as we don't want our time wasted, so we should remember that others too have a right to their time. Good conversations don't have to be lengthy. If we look back into our own lives we shall probably find that the conversations which we regard as decisive points in our careers, those conversations which changed us for the better in some special way, were not long ones. It may have been a mere sentence or two that went far to change our lives.

Finally, just as we have to avoid wasting time in long and fruitless conversations, so we must also beware of being too busy to take time for others. The excuse, "I don't have the time today," is often no more than a subterfuge, an escape device used because we do not really have the zeal or interest to help others. It is true that interruptions are sometimes bothersome, and there are days when we have to summon up all our patience to carry on a conversation; but very often God rewards our charity and patience by letting us see the good that was done in that particular conversation which we managed to squeeze in when we were busiest.

And a final tip! Should you find yourself the victim of some individual who seems merely to be wasting your conversational time, then forcefully turn the conversation to purely spiritual topics, the importance of saving one's soul, for instance. You'll soon find that either this person will show interest and you will see that your conversation is doing some good, or (more likely) he or she will depart, nevermore to return!

40

Conversational Snares

1st Prelude: Listen to the words of St. James about the use of our tongue: "With it we bless God the Father; and with it we curse men, who have been made after the likeness of God . . ."

2nd Prelude: Beg the grace to improve your conversational techniques so that you may bring greater benefits to those with whom you converse.

Just as conversation, whether used with a natural or a supernatural purpose, has rules which must be followed to make it successful and efficient, so too there are conversational snares to avoid. One of the first is this: we must not monopolize the conversation. If we do, it soon ceases to be a conversation—the dialogue is gone. What remains is a monologue, and there is no more deadly enemy of conversation.

A second thing to avoid is gossip. We must be careful to use the gift of communication which God has given us to build up not to tear down. Our power of speech must be used to help others not to destroy them. Sometimes religious persons can become quite careless in what they say about others. They pay no attention to the danger of serious sin involved in making such damaging statements. A reputation can be severely hurt by such carelessness, and those with whom we converse can be seriously scandalized by such remarks. The words of St. James in his epistle are frightening: "With it we bless God the Father; and with it we curse men, who have been made after the likeness of God. Out of the same mouth proceed blessing and cursing. These things, my brethren, ought not to be so" (James 3:9).

We are all busy people and our schedules are so full that we have to make our conversations necessarily brief. This can be an advantage because long conversations tend not only to be time wasters, but they prevent us from doing other duties and from conversing with others whom we may be able to benefit.

Above all we must try to be always kind and charitable in our conversations with others. This becomes particularly difficult when we have had a tiring day, for it often seems that the persons who come to consult us at the fag end of the day are often just those whose belligerent or rude attitudes try our patience most. (There are many virtues which can be learned through the practice of our conversational opportunities, and patience heads the list!)

We should always strive to speak well of others. It is told of Robert E. Lee that one day when an officer asked him how he could speak so highly of one of his bitterest enemies, a person who never missed the opportunity of maligning him, General Lee replied simply: "My friend, I was asked my opinion of him, not his opinion of me."

Let me carefully review the conversations I have had during the past week and honestly evaluate them for the benefit which they gave to others. Let me carefully note whether or not I may have fallen into some of the conversational snares. If so, let me plan how I shall avoid them in the future. Above all, let me frequently ask our Lord during my colloquies in this meditation that I may constantly improve my conversational abilities so that I may more efficiently bring his kingdom to the minds and hearts of those about me.

41

Our Lord's Conversation

1st Prelude: Picture to yourself our Lord conversing with the Samaritan woman by the well of Jacob.

2nd Prelude: Ask the grace to learn from and to imitate our Lord's power of conversation.

In considering the part that conversation can play in our apostolate, let us carefully think about the example which our Lord has given. His conversation with the Samaritan woman is a wonderful lesson; by means of it we can teach ourselves how to converse so that we may benefit others. First of all, let us carefully read the relatively lengthy account which St. John gives of this unusual conversation. The apostle pictures the scene for us simply and vividly. (John 4:3 ff.)

(Jesus) left Judea and went again into Galilee. Now he had to pass through Samaria. He came, accordingly, to a town of Samaria called Sichar, near the field that Jacob gave to his son Joseph. Now Jacob's well was there. Jesus therefore, wearied as he

was from the journey, was sitting at the well. It was
about the sixth hour. There came a Samaritan woman
to draw water.

We note that it was noon and that our Lord was tired.
The Samaritan woman comes and he asks her for a drink of
water from the well. Her reply seems a little contemptuous:
"How is it that thou, although thou art a Jew, dost ask drink
of me, who am a Samaritan woman?" For, as St. John
notes, "Jews do not associate with Samaritans." Our Lord is
not rebuffed by this reply but simply bypasses the contro-
versial issue to put the conversation upon quite another
plane. His promise of "living water" draws quite a different
sort of reply from her. "Sir, thou hast nothing to draw with,
and the well is deep. Whence then hast thou living water?
Art thou greater than our father Jacob . . . ?" Note the
sudden respect and change of tone; evidently this dull, sinful woman senses the greatness of our Lord. Then he kindly
explains to this chance passerby some of the wonderful
things in store for those who drink of the water which he
will give and how it will spring up "into life everlasting."

Now she begs for this water, and in answer to her request
our Lord suggests that she go call her husband. When she
replies, ambiguously, "I have no husband," he reveals his
full knowledge of her past sinful life and present miserable
moral state. The love of Christ for this lost sheep must have
been very evident in his words, for the woman was not
repelled; instead she tried to change the subject! "Sir, I see

thou art a prophet . . ." and she asked him about the place of true worship and the relationship between Jews and Samaritans on the question. The answer our Lord gave to her revealed more and more of God's eternal plan. Then when she affirmed her belief in the Messiah to come our Lord clearly told her that he was the Messiah! To this poor, sinful, "heretical" woman, he made the first recorded, clear manifestation of his real identity.

And he won an immediate disciple! "The woman therefore left her water-jar and went away into the town, and said to the people, 'Come and see a man who has told me all that I have ever done. Can he be the Christ?'"

There are a great many things for us to learn from this conversation of our Lord. First of all there is the manifest and striking kindness and love shown to this ignorant personality. Christ was worn out and hungry, and the woman, at first rather rude, throughout the conversation received the revelation with some quibbling. Our Lord was not discouraged but led her on slowly until she began at least to grasp some bits of the profound revelation which he was offering to her. His patience with her is remarkable. His picture of her moral state was true but kindly, and obviously she must have felt his love and mercy.

Let me quietly compare the various parts of this remarkable conversation with my own attitudes toward those who come to converse with me or with whom I have an opportunity to speak. Is my attitude kind and patient? Am I always striving to benefit others? When I impart knowledge is it to help others or to show my own riches? Does my conversational attitude change when I speak to those who are under my authority and then to those from whom I receive orders?

In my colloquies in this meditation let me go back time and again to the various episodes in this conversation between our Lord and the sinful Samaritan woman, and beg of him that I may imitate his ways. "I am the Way and the Truth and the Life."

42

Community Conversation

1st Prelude: Picture to yourself our Lord saying to the Samaritan woman, "He who drinks of the water that I will give him shall never thirst. . . ."

2nd Prelude: Ask for the grace to imitate our Lord's self-sacrifice in conversation.

When we are considering our attitudes toward conversation and the many opportunities conversation offers for the spreading of God's kingdom, we tend sometimes to think only about our conversations with outsiders, those who are not members of our religious community. Let me pause and consider the importance of conversations with those who share the *same Rule* and the *same ideals* as myself.

First of all, do I show an interest in their work and their plans, or do I find upon examination that my conversation with them invariably turns to *my* work and *my* interests? As an administrator do I show any interest in the teaching side of education? As a teacher do I attempt to show interest in the administrative work of those in my community? This interest in the work of the other members of the community will not only aid my conversation and help to make it of benefit to them, but it will prevent me from becoming completely and solely absorbed in my own little sphere.

A good technique to help develop one's interest in the work of others is to find out what they are doing. People are naturally pleased when an interest is taken in their work and when they find others asking about their successes and their plans. Usually even the most taciturn person can be brought into a conversation by inquiries about what he or she is doing and the things in which they are interested.

There are the many casual conversations, often on business matters, which I have with the other members of my community, but let me rather turn the spotlight upon the periods of "common recreation." The first question to face honestly is whether or not I consistently go to common recreation! If I do not, I can be sure right away that I am missing a great many opportunities of doing good to others. What is the real reason some religious constantly skip common recreation? Frankly, it is because recreation doesn't interest *them*. They "do not get anything out of it," as they say, so they stay away. In other words, their attitude is fundamentally a selfish one. They want to enjoy recreation without attempting to give anything in return. They are selfish—there is no other word for it.

Not interested in others, they do not see in common recreation an opportunity to benefit others, to learn more about the plans and ideals of those with whom they are working for the glory of God. As a consequence they never really learn a great deal about the members of their community; instead, they tend to become hermits within a community, and in modern religious organizations this is pretty much a contradiction in terms. Needless to say, such persons are missing a great many opportunities to do good to their neighbors, their literal neighbors, that is to say, the persons who live right next door to them!

Let me go over my own attitudes toward my conversational opportunities with the members of my own community. And let me be honest with myself. Do I go to recreation only to seek my own enjoyment? If I stay away from it, let me ask myself if the real reason does not lie in my own lack of generosity, my own failure to become interested in the work and plans of others, my own lack of real fraternal charity. In my colloquies during this meditation, let me think over the sentiments of Psalm 132: "Behold, how good it is, and how pleasant, where brethren dwell at one! . . . For there the Lord has pronounced his blessing, life forever."

43

Community Recreation

1st Prelude: Picture to yourself our Lord conversing with the Apostles at the Last Supper.

2nd Prelude: Ask for the grace to become ever more Christ-like in conversation.

Many of us have noticed in our counselling of others, in our contacts with our students and their parents, in our work as administrators, that some people seem to have a very different standard of politeness and conduct when they are outside their family circle. They seem to have a double standard: with outsiders they are careful to show themselves polite in conversation, circumspect in what they say and the way they say it; but when they come home they seem to take off this attitude with their overcoats. With justice we may point out to them the utter inconsistency of such an attitude.

And yet how goes it in our own religious life? Have we not noticed sometimes that our conduct with those outside the community is extremely polite and affable, while at home we seem at times barely civil? In our conversations with outsiders we are polite. We do not interrupt them. When we disagree, we disagree without being disagreeable. But at home! Let me carefully go over my conversations of the past week or two and see how many times I have failed in the respect and politeness which I surely owe to those of my community, even more than I owe to outsiders.

In the choice of those with whom I take my recreation—can I honestly say that I try to converse both with those whom I naturally find congenial as well as those with whom, because of differences in age or temperament, experience or education, I find the going considerably more difficult? If I carefully think over my attitudes, I will surely find that the root cause of such a discrepancy in my ability to converse and to benefit others by my conversation lies in a fundamental selfishness. I go to recreation merely to get what *I* can get out of it.

The choice of conversation is another facet of my dealings with others which I can well examine. Perhaps I notice that with outsiders, especially those who by reason of wealth or position are more important members of the local environment, I am most careful in my choice of subjects, I strive to adapt my conversation and interests to theirs. But when I inspect my attitudes toward those at home, at common recreation, I may find that I never think of choosing a topic which would be of special interest to another, or of presenting my questions in such a way as to draw out others' views and give them a chance to take part in the conversation.

It cannot be denied that conversation with others in religious life at times demands much more virtue than one would imagine. This is not unusual. Married people who are successful in marriage know very well the innumerable occasions when they must adapt their conversations and attitudes to those of their partner if they are to keep the family peace. One should not pretend that conversation with religious is always easy. It is not. But by our profession we claim to love God with our whole heart, mind, and strength, and *our neighbor as ourself*. Certainly, the members of our religious community are our closest neighbors!

Let me read over once more St. John's graphic description of our Lord's conversation with the Samaritan woman (John 4:3 ff.). And let me compare it with my own conversations—slowly, prayerfully, honestly.

44

Gratitude in My Life

1st Prelude: Picture to yourself our Lord saying sadly: "And where are the other nine? Were not ten made clean? But where are the other nine?" (Luke 17:17).

2nd Prelude: Ask sincerely that you may learn to be grateful.

Every now and then when we have done some little thing for a person, we may feel that he or she has not been sufficiently grateful to us. Perhaps there was not even a "thank you." Then we suddenly realize that ingratitude cuts *us* deeply. We are very conscious of a lack of gratitude when it comes our way, but do we ever pay much attention to our own lack of gratitude? Maybe we can say to ourselves that when people do us favors we are careful to say our "thank you." Do we act the same way in our dealings with God?

People naturally tend to take things for granted, and we know ourselves that very often those closest to us are the last to whom we pay thanks. It is not that we are ungrateful, we tell ourselves, but that we are forgetful. As children so often take their parents' love for granted, and husbands and wives become at times far too casual about the expression of gratitude within the family circle, so too it often seems to happen in religious life that we forget to thank God. For example, take up some of the meditation books or those for spiritual reading and check the indexes to see how often the subject of gratitude is treated. Not so very often! So it may be well for us to concentrate for a few days upon the importance of gratitude in our dealings with God.

First of all, let me note the presence (or absence) of gratitude in my own religious life. How often yesterday or during the last week did I thank God for the everyday gifts which he continually showers upon me? Let me just pause and check my prayers at Mass today and for the past several days. How often was a prayer of gratitude interspersed with the many prayers of petition which I made? There are prayers of gratitude in the framework of the Mass, in fact the great prayer of the Preface reminds me to thank God always and everywhere. If I strive to say the Preface with devotion and attention, I am sure that I have thanked God at least once during Mass!

But let me turn my attention to the other parts of my day as well. There is the opportunity of thanksgiving after meals which I sometimes perform so routinely, with my mind upon a dozen other things. Yet here is a good chance to work the virtue of gratitude into my life at least three times every day presuming that like most people I eat that often during the day! Then there is the examination of conscience which should certainly include a prayer of thanks, and dur-

ing the examination I should compare God's generosity
to me and mine to him.

Another means of determining the presence of gratitude
in my life is to check upon the visits I make to our Lord in
the Blessed Sacrament—what do I do at these visits? Do I
include a prayer of gratitude for God's favors to me or is
my usual attitude only one of demand and request, with no
thought of what has already been given?

As I review the various parts of my day in an honest
effort to determine whether I am fundamentally a grateful
or an ungrateful person to God, let me recall in my colloquies the sad words of our Lord, "And where are the
other nine?"

45

The Material Gifts God Gives Me

1st Prelude: Imagine to yourself our Lord saying sadly to you: "But where are the other nine?" (Luke 17:17).

2nd Prelude: Ask earnestly that today you may grow in gratitude to God for all that he has given you.

We have all often heard the phrase, "Count your blessings." This is indeed one way to make ourselves conscious of the many things for which we should be grateful each day. Even if we limit ourselves only to the material things about us, how grateful we should be!

There is first of all the fact that we have adequate housing and food. Think of the millions of people scattered throughout the vast lands of the Near East and Far East who have to plan so carefully each day in order to have enough food to live on! How many have to see their beloved families go without necessary food, to watch as their children become thin and diseased because they lack essential foods.

And yet each day *we* come to well-prepared and plentiful meals; each day we are usually the casual recipients of a well-balanced diet which so many millions cannot afford. Our rooms are adequate and generally well-protected from extremes of heat and cold. Our clothing is sufficient. How often during the past week or *even the past month* have I really thought about the "Thank you" I owe to God for so constantly giving me these necessities?

How quickly we become aware in counselling our students, or in conferring with others, of the drive for security. How often must we have noticed this in the lay people who work with us, in the teachers and administrators we have met, in the young people who come to us for guidance. This desire and planning for security becomes more dominant as they grow older, for then people begin to worry more and more about it.

And what of ourselves? The greatest security is constantly ours. Day after day we are cared for, we possess in abundance the very security which those outside the religious life are so anxious to obtain. And as we grow older the proofs of this security become even clearer. No expense is spared to see that we are kept in good health, and if sickness visits us we are given the best medical and hospital care. When we grow old and feeble (presumably in God's service), we need never fear of being cast out, of having to live aloof and alone as so many old people around us. As a member of a religious order or congregation, we share the greatest built-in plan of old-age security that the world has ever seen.

All of these material things have been given to us so

consistently, so effortlessly, that we take them for granted. Seldom, if ever, do we think about them. But let the cook be five or ten minutes late, or the heat suddenly go off for a few hours, and there may ensue considerable unrest in the monastic roost! Isn't it a shame that we sometimes only think of the things we have been given when we suddenly find we have to do without them? And yet all day long, God our loving Father is constantly showering his benefits upon us. We tend so naturally to take all of his gifts for granted, and as a result we forget to thank God for all the material things he gives us each hour, each minute of the day.

Let us recall the proverb: "I complained because I had no shoes until I met a man who had no feet."

46

God's Intellectual Gifts to Me

1st Prelude: Recall the grateful man out of whom Jesus had cast the devils. "And he departed, and began to publish in the Decapolis all that Jesus had done for him. And all marveled." (Mark 5:20)

2nd Prelude: Ask for the grace to understand and be grateful for the many intellectual benefits which God has given to you in particular.

How often have we thought of the various intellectual helps and safeguards which God has given us, especially those which he gave us before we entered religion? Our grade school and high school life, the many good and sincerely devoted teachers we have had, the good companions, the helpful classes, the sincere counselling, the general intellectual atmosphere which helped rather than hindered our deepening faith, hope, and charity. And of course we must not forget the role of our parents. In how many cases parents who themselves did not have a high school or college education scrimped and saved in order that their children might have such benefits. "How shall I make a return to the Lord for all the good he has done for me?" (Ps. 115:3)

Most of us tend to think back on our novitiate days as a time when we were rather inexperienced and tended to scramble along the road of perfection in a clumsy way, perhaps without much prudence. Still, we should never forget that most of the principles which were henceforth to guide and spur us on to our better moments in the religious life came from the educational processes of this rigorous training. The amount of reading and prayer we did then aided greatly in impressing upon our minds the general attitudes that we have carried through life. We learned a great many things that millions of God's creatures have never even had an opportunity of hearing. The novitiate was really a school, an educational process which changed our whole outlook on things whether we then realized it or not.

As we advanced in our training, most of us were given the equivalent of a college education and some were sent on to graduate studies in special fields. Generally we had between five and ten years of training counting postulancy and novitiate. In financial figures that would represent a $15,000 to $20,000 education considering the cost of higher education today. These are benefits of a special type, and there are untold millions of people in our world who could never possibly hope to obtain such an education. And yet what have we done about thanking God for his constant giving?

Another part of God's intellectual gifts to me consists in the opportunity to increase my knowledge both of intellectual and spiritual matters. The constant spiritual reading, even if only for a few minutes each day, mounts up from week to week and year to year into the equivalent of a number of collegiate courses in asceticism, if I have chosen my books well and wisely. Then too there is the constant companionship of those doing work of a like nature to my own. Only those who have had community life in an educational institution and then have had to go it alone, perhaps by reason of a special assignment or because of sickness, can really appreciate the educational and intellectual benefits which such community living provides. Again it is the same failing. We cannot really seem to appreciate such gifts until we have been deprived of them!

Let me slowly say the words of Psalm 144 and make their sentiments my own.

> I will extol you, O my God and King, and I will bless your name forever and ever. Every day will I bless you and I will praise your name forever and ever. . . . The Lord is gracious and merciful . . . The Lord is good to all and compassionate toward all his works. Let all your works give you thanks, O Lord, and let your faithful ones bless you. . . . The Lord is faithful in all his words and holy in all his works . . . The Lord is near to all who call upon him. . . . he hears their cry and saves them. The Lord keeps all who love him . . . May my mouth speak the praise of the Lord and may all flesh bless his holy name forever and ever.

47

God's Spiritual Gifts to Me

1st Prelude: Listen to our Lord saying sadly: "Has no one been found to return and give glory to God except this foreigner?" (Luke 17:18)

2nd Prelude: Ask for the grace to appreciate and to be grateful for the spiritual gifts God gives you today.

As we know so well, the religious life makes it easier for us to fulfill more completely in our lives the will of God. In doing the will of God consists our perfection. But to do his will better each day, we need more and more of his help and grace which we get through our use of prayer and the sacraments. Among the sacraments, two are continually helpful to us—the sacraments of Penance and Holy Eucharist.

Did I ever stop to think how relatively easy it is for me to make use of these two all-important sacraments? In many parts of the world Catholics cannot get to a church easily. Governments or a dearth of priests can make it almost impossible for them to get to the sacraments at all. Even in my own city or town, if I compare the ease with which I can go to frequent confession and daily Mass and Communion with the case of the average Catholic, how thankful I should be! Often God lives in the same house with me and I do not even have to go outside on a cold morning to visit him. These opportunities have been in my life, my religious life, perhaps for a great many years, and yet how often have I thanked God for them? Let me think often of these words of Holy Scripture: "Give thanks to the Lord, for he is good, for his mercy endures forever" (Dan. 3:89).

If I were to count all the spiritual blessings that our Lord each day offers to me, how surprised would I be at their numbers. There is the daily spiritual reading which increases my knowledge and love of God and thus, too, my everlasting happiness. There are the various conversations which I have with members of my community, these persons who have the same ideals as my own, who together with me desire to do God's will. And, of course, there are the various opportunities which God gives me each day to do apostolic work for him, to further his kingdom upon earth. Were I to investigate carefully each of the many gifts which will come to me today alone and then begin to thank God for them, I would surely find that the time of this meditation would not be sufficient to cover them all.

Consider the great opportunities of liturgical worship which God gives to me each day. How many millions in the world today cannot get to Mass; how many more do not even know what the Mass means! Yet each and every day, despite my lack of cooperation, despite my casual acceptance of such a great gift, God continues to make it so easy for me to perform this great act of praise and thanksgiving.

I should not blind myself to the danger of such a casual acceptance of these benefits, to the possibility that my lack of gratitude for such great and continual giving may greatly displease our Lord. I have but to think of how I feel when students or subordinates do not seem duly appreciative of some minor thing I have done for them, with what difficulty I keep my patience in the face of some small evidence of ingratitude. Then let me consider my own actions toward God. Recall the advice of St. Paul: "In all things give thanks; for this is the will of God in Christ Jesus regarding you all" (I Thess. 5:18). Do I strive to follow this?

Let me recite slowly in my colloquies of this meditation the following verses from Psalm 12: "Let my heart rejoice in your salvation. Let me sing of the Lord, 'He has been good to me.' "

48

The Mass—My Thanksgiving Prayer

1st Prelude: Imagine yourself present with the Apostles and our Lord at the Last Supper. "And having taken bread, he gave thanks. . . ." (Luke 22:19)

2nd Prelude: Ask the grace that you may always offer your Mass in deep gratitude for all the gifts God has given to you, to your religious community, and to your religious order or congregation.

Very possibly the thought may have occurred to us that at the time of our own particular judgment one of the key questions which our Lord will ask is this one: "Why didn't you thank me?"

Now there are many opportunities during the day when I can thank God for all that he has given me up to that very minute, but one of the most important times is at Mass. The Mass is a eucharistic offering, that is, in the original Greek meaning, a thank-you offering to God. How often the various prayers of the Mass—both those which change from day to day and those which are said each day—how often these prayers are prayers of gratitude to God. If only I didn't skip over them so carelessly! For here is the great opportunity every day to make sure that I *do* thank our Lord for all he has done for me. And most certainly I want to make sure that I shall not hear the terrifying words of Deuteronomy spoken to me:

> Yet basely has he been treated by his degenerate children, a perverse and crooked race! Is the Lord to be thus repaid by you, O stupid and foolish people? Is he not your father who created you? Has he not made you and established you? Think back on the days of old . . . (32:5)

Let me page through my missal and note the many prayers of thanksgiving which I normally recite *each* day, and let me reflect whether or not I normally use these prayers to express my own gratitude for the special gifts which God has been giving to me. Often I shall find such prayers of gratitude in the Introit or the Gradual and, of course, at the Communion song and the Prayer after Communion.

The greatest thanksgiving prayer of the Mass, however, as we all know, is the Preface. There with a solemn introduction together with the celebrant we thank our Lord for all that has been given to us. We remember that each major feast and season has its own special Preface, but the one with which we are perhaps most familiar is the Common Preface, the one which is said most of the time during the liturgical year. Let us go through that Preface slowly and see how it can become our daily great "Thank You" prayer, thus making us more sure that we are fulfilling our duty of gratitude to God.

> ... Let us thank the Lord our God.
> It is meet and right to do so.
> Truly it is meet and right, it is our duty, it is our salvation to thank you always and everywhere, to thank you, Lord holy father, God almighty and everlasting, through Christ our Lord. Through him the Angels praise your majesty, the Dominations worship it and the Powers of the heaven tremble. The hosts of heaven join with the holy Seraphim in a hymn of celebration. We ask that our voice may join in too as all together we sing out joyfully our humble proclamation. Holy, Holy, Holy, ...

Let me examine my understanding and practical application of such thoughts. May my daily attendance at Mass become my chief profession of gratitude toward God! What have I been doing about this? What am I doing about it? What shall I do about it?

49

Opportunities for Gratitude

1st Prelude: Let me picture to myself the Apostle St. John as he writes these words: "In this is the love, not that we have loved God, but that he has first loved us, and sent his son as a propitiation for our sins" (I John 4:10).

2nd Prelude: Ask the grace that today you may make good use of the opportunities you have for thanking God.

Doubtless one of the aspects of our life which will strike us most sharply when it is over and we are being judged is the number of opportunities in our everyday lives which slipped by us. For instance, in the matter of being grateful to God for the many things which he is constantly giving me, how many times during the course of my ordinary day am I given an opportunity of thanking him!

There are the prayers of grace at meals. Three times each day I say prayers of thanksgiving, but what do they generally mean to me and in what manner do I say such prayers? At the time of my examination of conscience I find a part of this devoted to thanking God for his benefits to me—what use do I generally make of this opportunity?

During the prayers of the Office which I recite, how often do the sentiments of thanksgiving come up in the psalms and responses, the prayers and readings, and how often do I use these opportunities to thank God for what he is giving me today? How carefully do I pray them?

Then too there are the various vocal prayers which I say during the day, my rosary, for example. How often do I offer such prayers in thanks to God? The several visits to the Blessed Sacrament which I customarily make during the course of the day—am I always asking for things and never giving thanks?

We all admit that thanksgiving should form a considerable portion of our life of that adoration and praise to God which, after all, is the purpose of our lives, the reason why we have accepted God's invitation to a religious life. We all know and believe that this is so, but how much of this belief do we carry into our lives each day? And how much use do we make of all the many opportunities which are given to us so generously? We have been taught from our novitiate days, and we have often read the same in our spiritual reading through the years, that it is not in many extra prayers, not in the addition of many devotions, but in the perfect fulfillment of the various duties of our everyday lives that we are to find our perfection. In this *routine* lies our perfection. And it is precisely in such a routine that we find so many opportunities to show our Lord our thankfulness.

Let me think about the way I have been making use of these opportunities; for if I do not carefully consider my ordinary routine, I shall certainly not remedy the situation. And throughout this meditation let me make the sentiments of Psalm 17 my own.

I love thee, O Lord, my strength, O Lord, my rock, my fortress, my deliverer . . . Praised be the Lord, I exclaim, and I am safe from my enemies. . . . In my distress I called upon the Lord and cried out to my God; From his temple he heard my voice, and my cry to him reached his ears. . . . He reached out from on high and grasped me; he drew me out of the deep waters. He rescued me from my mighty enemy . . . and rescued me, because he loves me.

And those of Psalm 64:

To you we owe our hymn of praise, O God, in Zion; to you must vows be fulfilled, you who hear prayers. To you all flesh must come because of wicked deeds. We are overcome by our sins; it is you who pardon them. Happy the man you choose, and bring to dwell in your courts. May we be filled with the good things of your house, the holy things of your temple!

50

Saving My Soul

1st Prelude: Listen to our Lord saying these words to you personally: "The kingdom of Heaven suffereth violence and the violent bear it away" (Matt. 11:12).

2nd Prelude: Beg our Lord to show you simply and clearly what your real attitudes are.

Did you ever meet a man or woman *really* interested in a project? They are always working at it. They are always talking it over with others. They are always seeking advice about it. They bore us with their plans, their ideas, their decisions. They don't notice many other things. They are concentrating their attention on their project. They are really interested in that one thing.

Let me ask myself: Do I ever think much about saving my soul? Isn't that the first and only necessary thing for everyone to do? Don't I tell this to others, to my pupils, to the people I advise and influence? Do I tell it to myself? What is my first thought upon awaking in the morning? Does this ever occur to me then?

We learn to think about important things by actually

thinking about them. We tell others of the importance of thinking about good things, important things, things of the soul, because the thoughts and trends of thought which one cultivates will come back from force of habit for good or evil. Have I been cluttering up my mind with useless, vain, frivolous or perhaps even dangerous things? How would our Lord evaluate the thoughts that normally occupy my mind? If I lined up all the things that I have thought about today, how often would I find myself thinking about my soul and its safety—or the souls of others? Perhaps he would have to speak to me as he did to Martha: "Thou art anxious and troubled about many things; and yet only one thing is needful . . ." (Luke 10:41).

Let me briefly tell our Lord what I would like to think about. Let me resolve to think today at least about the importance of saving my own soul. Let me also recall two or three times during this day the words: "What does it profit a man, if he gain the whole world, but suffer the loss of his own soul? Or what will a man give in exchange for his soul?" (Matt. 16:26). Do I honestly believe this?

51

The Praise of All

1st Prelude: Recall to mind the famous words of Dante: "In His will is our peace—*E in la sua volontade è nostra pace*" (*Paradiso*, iii/85).

2nd Prelude: Beg for an ever-deepening understanding of the true purpose of life—"to praise, reverence and serve God in this life and to be happy with him forever in the next."

Despite the din of everyday life which drums so loudly into our ears that we cannot always keep our recollection, we know deep within ourselves that it is only God and the doing of his will that matters. And it is precisely the knowledge of this solid principle that gives us lasting peace of mind. As we think upon this truth, let us remember that truly each day, each hour of our lives has been dedicated to the doing of his will. Our prayers and our work, our conversations and hours of study, our class lectures and our committee meetings, all are but the fulfillment of his will in our lives.

And in all these matters we are continually praising God!

As we have to tell ourselves over and over again, it is in such routine matters that our perfection lies. The warp and woof of our daily lives is made of such items and the over-all picture of our lives will be but the tapestry woven of them. We must constantly impress upon ourselves the importance of these common, run-of-the-mill events, because unless we do we shall miss the great opportunities of our lives. Too late we shall come to recognize that our lives consisted of such everyday occurrences, and we completely misunderstood their importance.

So we must constantly emphasize to ourselves that throughout our day we are praising, reverencing, and serving God in all these everyday affairs. We are doing his will. And in this lies our true objective, in the perfection of such things lies the true greatness of our lives. There too we find our peace of mind. "Those who love your law have great peace, and for them there is no stumbling block." (Ps. 118:165)

So then, amidst the constant ebb and flow of the many things we have to do each day we must learn to preserve ourselves in peace. We must constantly remind ourselves of the great principle which should dominate all we do, the maxim that should rule all aspects of our lives—the will of God; "Thy will be done" as we pray so often in the Our Father. Such an attitude is essential in our busy lives if we are to secure the peace which Christ wishes us to have. We affirm our desire in our morning prayers, in our Morning Offering of doing God's will in our lives that very day.

During many other occasions in our day, in the routine prayers which we say, in the visits to the chapel which we make, we have many opportunities to renew this desire, this basic aim of our lives.

Each time we pray for this, we strengthen its efficacy in our lives, we deepen our understanding of this most important truth—that in doing God's will consists the perfection of our lives. Not in dreams of grandiose, future labors and deeds which are often only castles in the air, but in the humdrum duties of *this morning* and *this afternoon* do we fulfill his wishes. And in doing these things as well as we can, we offer to God the great acts of praise of our lives, indeed our lives become continual acts of praise to him.

Let me use Psalm 148 to express my thoughts to our Lord during my colloquies in this meditation.

Praise the Lord from the heavens, praise him in the heights; praise him all you his angels, praise him, all you his hosts. . . . Let the kings of the earth and all the peoples, the princes and all the judges of the earth, young men too, and maidens, old men and boys, praise the name of the Lord, for his name alone is exalted; his majesty is above earth and heaven . . .